# Optimi

# Tort Law

# OPTIMIZE LAW REVISION

Titles in the series:
Contract Law
Equity and Trusts
Land Law
Public Law
EU Law
Tort Law

The Optimize series' academic advisors are:

– Michael Bromby, Higher Education Academy Discipline Lead for Law 2011–2013, Reader in Law at Glasgow Caledonian University.

'The use of visualisation in Optimize will help students to focus on the key issues when revising.'

– Emily Allbon, Senior Lecturer in Law and creator of Lawbore, City University.

'Partnering well-explained, comprehensive content with visual tools like maps and flowcharts is what makes the Optimize series so unique. These books help students take their learning up a notch; offering support in grappling with the subject, as well as insight into what will help make their work stand out.'

– Sanmeet Kaur Dua, Lecturer in Law, co-creator of Lawbore, City University.

'This series sets out the essential concepts and principles that students need to grasp in a logical way by combining memorable visual diagrams and text. Students will find that they will not easily forget what they read in this series as the unique aim higher and interaction points will leave a blueprint in their minds.'

– Zoe Swan, Senior Lecturer in Law, University of Greenwich.

'The wide range of visual material includes diagrams, charts, tables and maps to enable students to check their knowledge and understanding on each topic area, every step of the way … When combined with carefully explained legal principles and solid, understandable examples, students will find this series provides them with a win-win solution to the study of law and developing revision techniques.'

# Optimize
# Tort Law

**Brendan Greene**

Routledge
Taylor & Francis Group

LONDON AND NEW YORK

First published 2017
by Routledge
2 Park Square, Milton Park, Abingdon, Oxon OX14 4RN

and by Routledge
711 Third Avenue, New York, NY 10017

*Routledge is an imprint of the Taylor & Francis Group, an informa business*

*British Library Cataloguing in Publication Data*
A catalogue record for this book is available from the British Library

*Library of Congress Cataloging in Publication Data*
Names: Greene, Brendan, author.
Title: Optimize tort law/Brendan Greene.
Description: New York: Routledge, 2017. | Series: Optimize | Includes index.
Identifiers: LCCN 2016040969 | ISBN 9781138221512 (pbk.) |
ISBN 9781315410258(e-book)
Subjects: LCSH: Torts–Great Britain.
Classification: LCC KD1949 .G69 2017 | DDC 346.4103–dc23
LC record available at https://lccn.loc.gov/2016040969

ISBN: 978-1-138-22151-2 (pbk)
ISBN: 978-1-315-41025-8 (ebk)

Typeset in TheSans
by Wearset Ltd, Boldon, Tyne and Wear
Printed and bound by CPI Group (UK) Ltd, Croydon, CR0 4YY

**Visit the companion website: www.routledge.com/cw/optimizelawrevision**

# Contents

# Optimize – Your Blueprint for Exam Success

## Why Optimize?

In developing the 'Optimize' format, Routledge have spent a lot of time talking to law lecturers and examiners about assessment, teaching and learning and exam preparation. The aim of our series is to help you make the most of your knowledge to gain good marks – to optimize your revision.

## Students

Students told us that there was a huge amount to learn and that visual features such as diagrams, tables and flowcharts made the law easier to follow. Learning and remembering cases was an area of difficulty, as was applying these in problem questions. Revision guides could make this easier by presenting the law succinctly, showing concepts in a visual format and highlighting how important cases can be applied in assessment.

## Lecturers

Lecturers agreed that visual features were effective to aid learning, but were concerned that students learned by rote when using revision guides. To succeed in assessment, they wanted to encourage them to get their teeth into arguments, to support their answers with authority and to show they had truly understood the principles underlying their questions. In short, they wanted them to show they understood how they were assessed on the law, rather than repeating the basic principles.

## Assessment criteria

If you want to do well in exams, it's important to understand how you will be assessed. In order to get the best out of your exam or essay question, your first port of call should be to make yourself familiar with the marking criteria available from your law school; this will help you to identify and recognise the skills and knowledge you will need to succeed. Like course outlines, assessment criteria can differ from school to school and so if you can get hold of a copy of your own criteria, this will be invaluable. To give you a clear idea of what these criteria look like, we've collated the most common terms from 64 marking schemes for core curriculum courses in the UK.

research
reading
Evidence
Understanding
Structure  Engagement  Critical Argument  sources
Analysis  Application  Use
Accuracy  Originality
Knowledge
Presentation

*Common Assessment Criteria, Routledge Subject Assessment Survey*

## Optimizing the law

The format of this 'Optimize Law' volume has been developed with these assessment criteria and the learning needs of students firmly in mind.

❖ **Visual format:** Our expert series advisors have brought a wealth of knowledge about visual learning to help us to develop the books' visual format.

❖ **Tailored coverage:** Each book is tailored to the needs of your core curriculum course and presents all commonly taught topics.

❖ **Assessment led-revision:** Our authors are experienced teachers with an interest in how students learn, and they have structured each chapter around revision objectives that relate to the criteria you will be assessed on.

❖ **Assessment led-pedagogy:** The 'Aim Higher', 'Common Pitfalls', 'Up for Debate' and 'Case Precedent' features used in these books are closely linked to common assessment criteria – showing you how to gain the best marks, avoid the worst pitfalls, apply the law and think critically about it.

❖ **Putting it into practice:** Each chapter presents example essays or problem questions and template answers to show you how to apply what you have learned.

Routledge and the 'Optimize' team wish you the very best of luck in your exams and essays!

# Guide to Using the Book and the Companion Website

The Routledge 'Optimize' revision series is designed to provide students with a clear overview of the core topics in their course, and to contextualise this overview within a narrative that offers straightforward, practical advice relating to assessment.

## Revision objectives

A brief introduction to the core themes and issues you will encounter in each chapter.

## Chapter Topic Maps

Visually link all of the key topics in each chapter to tie together understanding of key issues.

## Illustrative diagrams

A series of diagrams and tables are used to help facilitate the understanding of concepts and interrelationships within key topics.

## Up for Debate

'Up for Debate' helps you to critique current law and reflect on how and in which direction it may develop in the future.

## Case precedent boxes

A variety of landmark cases are highlighted in text boxes for ease of reference. The facts, principle and application for the case are presented to help understand how these courses are used in legal problems.

## Aim Higher and Common Pitfalls

These assessment-focused sections show students how to get the best marks, and avoid the most common mistakes.

# Table of key cases

Drawing together the key cases from each chapter.

# Companion Website

www.routledge.com/cw/optimizelawrevision

Visit the Law Revision website to discover a comprehensive range of resources designed to enhance your learning experience.

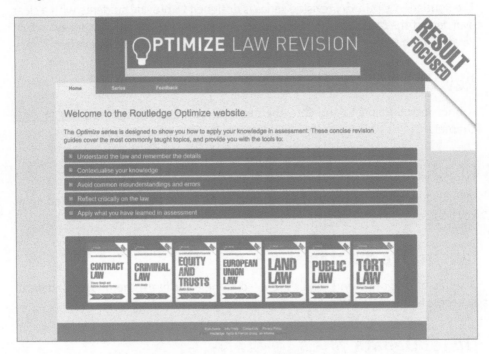

# Resources for Optimize Law revision

❖ Revision tips podcasts
❖ Topic overview podcasts
❖ Subject maps for each topic
❖ Downloadable versions of Chapter Maps and other diagrams
❖ Flashcard Glossary
❖ MCQ questions

# Table of Cases and Statutes

## ■ Cases

# ■ Statutes and statutory instruments

## ■ European and international legislation

# 1

# Negligence: Duty of Care

## Revision objectives

**Understand the law**
- Can you outline the three requirements to establish a duty of care in negligence?
- Can you explain the general rule on liability in negligence for omissions and the exceptions to it?
- Can you explain the circumstances when someone is liable in negligence for the acts of third parties?
- Can you explain the legal position of local authorities in negligence?

**Remember the details**
- Can you explain the test of foreseeability in negligence?
- Can you explain proximity using cases to illustrate your answer?
- Can you explain the liability of the police in negligence?
- Can you distinguish between the liability of the fire and ambulance services in negligence?

**Reflect critically on areas of debate**
- Can you explain the expansion of the duty of care and the later approach of development by incremental steps?
- Can you explain the difficulties of suing the police for negligence?

**Contextualise**
- Do you understand how foreseeability, proximity and just, fair and reasonableness work together to either restrict or expand the duty of care?
- Do you understand how policy is used in determining if a duty of care exists?

**Apply your skills and knowledge**
- Can you answer the essay question at the end of this chapter?

# Chapter Map

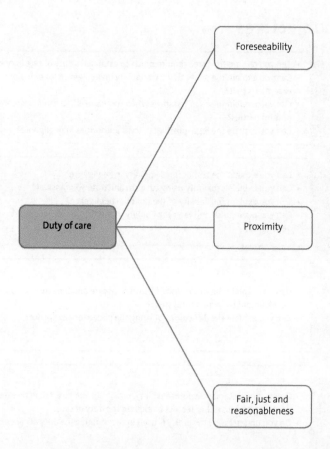

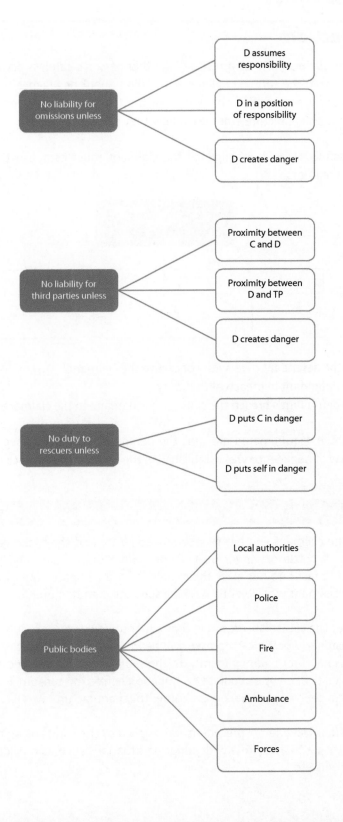

# Introduction

If someone suffers harm as a result of another person's careless act they may be able to claim in the tort of negligence. Learning about negligence is like doing a jigsaw puzzle because it is only when all the 'pieces' of negligence have been studied that a clear picture emerges of how they all fit together.

To successfully claim in negligence the claimant must establish the following three requirements.

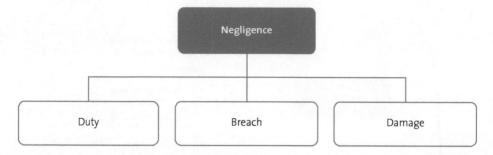

- ❖ Does the defendant owe a duty of care to the claimant?
- ❖ Is the defendant in breach of that duty?
- ❖ Is the defendant's breach the cause of the damage to the claimant?

If these three requirements are met the defendant is liable in negligence. The modern law of negligence was established in the following famous case.

---

### Case precedent – *Donoghue v Stevenson* [1932] AC 562

**Facts:** The claimant and her friend went to a café and the friend bought the claimant a bottle of ginger beer. The claimant drank some and when she poured the rest into her glass the remains of a snail floated out of the bottle and the claimant was violently sick. She sued the manufacturer for negligence.

**Principle:** The House of Lords held that a manufacturer owes a duty of care to the consumer who he can foresee will be injured if the product is defective. The manufacturer had negligently let the snail into the bottle and there was no possibility of an intermediate examination before the consumer drank it as the ginger beer was in a dark glass bottle. The manufacturer was liable.

**Application:** The original precedent was applied by the courts using the neighbour principle to apply to a wide range of situations such as providers of services, drivers etc.

In *Donoghue v Stevenson* Lord Atkin set out the neighbour principle.

> 'You must take reasonable care to avoid acts or omissions which you can reasonably foresee would be likely to injure your neighbour. Who then in law is my neighbour? The answer seems to be persons who are so closely and directly affected by my act that I ought reasonably to have them in contemplation as being so affected when I am directing my mind to the acts or omissions which are called in question.'

# The development of negligence

*Donoghue v Stevenson* created a general principle of liability for negligence, the neighbour principle. In the years after this the courts gradually extended the principle to cover new duty situations. In *Carmarthenshire County Council v Lewis* [1955] AC 549 a four year old child left the school through an unlocked gate, and walked 90 metres down the road before running in front of a lorry causing it to crash and kill the driver. There was proximity between the council and the driver and the council had control of the child. They owed a duty of care to the driver and were liable in negligence.

In *Home Office v Dorset Yacht Co* [1970] AC 1004 Lord Reid made the following statement about the neighbour principle,

> 'I think that the time has come when we can and should say that it ought to apply unless there is some justification or valid explanation for its exclusion.'

Lord Reid was saying that in new situations the 'neighbour principle' should apply unless there was a reason why it should not apply. This was an attempt to create a single general principle to be used to determine whether a duty of care was owed in negligence.

The courts used this approach to expand the tort of negligence during the 1970s and 1980s. In *Anns v Merton London Borough Council* [1977] 2 All ER 492 Lord Wilberforce refined this single principle into a two-stage test.

**Stage 1**

Is there a relationship of proximity between the claimant and defendant such that the defendant ought to contemplate that his careless act will cause harm to the claimant?

If the answer is 'yes' then a second question is asked.

**Stage 2**

Are there any factors which would end the duty or restrict it?

If the answer to this question is 'no', then a duty of care is owed.

In *Caparo v Dickman* [1990] 1 All ER 568 in the House of Lords Lord Bridge said that the courts were moving away from the search for a single general principle of negligence. He cited Brennan J from the Australian case of *Sutherland Shire Council v Heyman* (1985) 157 CLR 424:

'the law should develop novel categories of negligence incrementally and by analogy with established categories, rather than by a massive extension of a prima facie duty of care restrained only by indefinable considerations which ought to negative or to reduce or limit the scope of the duty or the class of the person to whom it is owed.'

This approach is to develop negligence 'step by step' through using existing precedents.

In *Caparo* the House of Lords moved away from the search for a single general principle which could be used to establish a duty of care. It also changed from the assumption a duty was owed unless there was a good reason why not, to the position where a duty had to be established. The effect of this was to restrict the development and expansion of negligence.

## Common Pitfall

When answering problem questions apply the three-stage test of duty from *Caparo*. The two-stage Wilberforce test and Lord Reid's attempt to have a one stage general test for duty of care are only relevant to questions on the history or development of negligence.

# Duty of care

Lord Bridge set out a three-stage test for establishing whether a duty of care existed.

This became the universal test to establish a duty of care. All three requirements have to be met. The three requirements are not mutually exclusive and there are relationships and overlaps between them. For example, if something is foreseeable there is also a greater chance there will be a relationship of proximity. The test is used for all types of harm including physical damage, injury, psychiatric harm or economic loss.

## Foreseeability

The test of foreseeability is: could the reasonable person, in the defendant's position, have reasonably foreseen that the claimant would have been injured if the defendant did the particular act?

This test involves the concept of the reasonable person (formerly the 'reasonable man') which is an objective test of the defendant's actions, that means, it is looked at from an outside point of view.

This is in contrast to a subjective test which would ask whether the individual defendant would have foreseen the harm to the claimant. If a subjective test were applied the defendant could simply say that they did not foresee the harm and no duty would be owed.

In *Bourhill v Young* [1942] 2 All ER 396 the claimant, a pregnant Edinburgh fish seller, was getting off a tram when she heard an accident. The defendant was speeding on his motorcycle, collided with a car and was killed. The accident happened 15 metres away behind another tram. The claimant saw blood on the road and later suffered nervous shock and had a miscarriage. She sued for negligence. The House of Lords held that it was not reasonably foreseeable that someone so far away would suffer nervous shock and no duty of care was owed.

## Common Pitfall

The test of foreseeability is a reasonable person in the defendant's position and not whether the defendant could foresee that if they acted in a particular way the claimant would suffer harm.

## Proximity

The word proximity means nearness or closeness. The legal term 'proximity of relationship' derives from Lord Atkin's neighbour principle. The claimant needs to prove proximity of relationship with the defendant and this may be done by proving physical closeness, closeness of relationship or a policy reason. It may also be a combination of these factors.

If the defendant is physically close to the claimant it is more likely there will be proximity. For example, if the defendant is practising shots with a golf club a couple of metres away from another person, there will be proximity of relationship with that person.

A closeness of relationship may be established by the nature of the relationship. The degree of closeness required will depend on the type of damage, for example, a claim for financial loss or psychiatric injury needs a very close relationship.

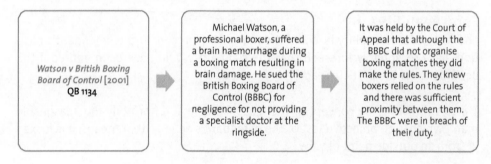

*Watson v British Boxing Board of Control* [2001] **QB 1134** ➡ Michael Watson, a professional boxer, suffered a brain haemorrhage during a boxing match resulting in brain damage. He sued the British Boxing Board of Control (BBBC) for negligence for not providing a specialist doctor at the ringside. ➡ It was held by the Court of Appeal that although the BBBC did not organise boxing matches they did make the rules. They knew boxers relied on the rules and there was sufficient proximity between them. The BBBC were in breach of their duty.

Another factor which the courts consider is policy. Generally the courts make decisions by using legal principles and precedents. Courts may also make decisions for policy reasons. A policy reason is a non-legal reason for making a decision. Policy reasons may be used to create a duty or to prevent a duty arising. Policy reasons cover a wide range of things including the following examples:

- ❖ The floodgates argument: making the defendant liable would lead to lots of claims, so the court would find the defendant does not owe a duty.
- ❖ The claim would be paid from public funds: therefore the defendant should not be liable.
- ❖ The defendant has insurance and is able to pay: so the defendant should be liable.
- ❖ No duty owed if it would apply to an indeterminate class of people: so that millions of people would owe a duty.

There has always been disagreement among judges on the use of policy. In *McLoughlin v O'Brian* [1983] AC 410 Lord Scarman said that the objective of the judges was the formulation of principle not policy. Yet in the same case Lord Edmund-Davies took the opposite view. One argument against the use of policy is that it makes the law uncertain. However, one of the main benefits of using policy is that it enables the law to change and adapt with the times, for example, see *Arthur Hall v Simons* [2000] 3 All ER 673 which allowed barristers acting in court to be sued for negligence.

---

**Case precedent – *Hill v Chief Constable of West Yorkshire* [1988] 2 All ER 238**

**Facts:** The mother of the last victim of the 'Yorkshire Ripper' sued the police for negligence, on behalf of her daughter's estate, claiming that the police should have arrested him earlier and prevented her daughter's murder.

**Principle:** The daughter was one of many women at risk and there was no proximity of relationship between her and the police. The House of Lords also took into account policy reasons that if the police were made liable they would worry about people suing them. This would lead to them adopting defensive policing practices and to diverting resources to deal with claims. The court said that in the investigation and suppression of crime the police did not owe a duty of care in negligence.

**Application:** The *Hill* principle which is that the police do not owe a duty of care to individual members of the public has been applied in many cases since, for example, *Smith v Chief Constable of Sussex* [2008] page 16.

---

In *Osman v Ferguson* [1993] 4 All ER 344 a teacher, P, began to pester the claimant, a 15 year old pupil at his school. P followed the boy around and told the police that he would do something mad. P went to the boy's house and shot dead the boy's father and injured the boy. The boy sued the police for negligence. It was argued that there was a close proximity between the family and the police because they were known to the police. But it was held applying *Hill* that the claim should be 'struck out' and that the police did not owe a duty of care to the boy because it would mean diverting resources.

The family subsequently brought a claim to the European Court of Human Rights in *Osman v United Kingdom* (1998) 29 EHRR 245. It was then held that refusing to hear the case was a breach of Article 6 the right to a fair hearing and the family were awarded damages.

## Fair, just and reasonableness
If a claimant establishes foreseeability and proximity a court may still find that in all the circumstances it is not 'fair, just and reasonable' to impose a duty on the defendant.

This requirement gives the courts flexibility to deny a duty exists if, on balance, it seems reasonable to do so. Examples of this are the cases of *Mulcahy v Ministry of Defence* [1996] 2 WLR 474 and *Smith v Ministry of Defence* [2013] UKSC 41 below.

## Comment on the requirements for duty

These three requirements are not distinct tests and they must be seen in relation to each other, for example, if there is proximity it is more likely to be just and reasonable to owe a duty. They must also be seen in relation to the function or purpose of the duty of care in negligence which is to determine the boundaries of liability. Each one of the factors is quite general and leaves room for debate as to exactly what they mean. Policy reasons are traditionally seen as only relevant to fair, just and reasonableness but in practice policy may be used in relation to all three factors.

### Up For Debate

In examining the use of policy in establishing a duty the courts are trying to balance factors in favour of the public interest and the right of the claimant to a remedy. Read the case of *Michael v Chief Constable of South Wales Police* [2015] UKSC 2 which was a 5/2 majority decision of the Supreme Court especially the dissenting judgments of Lord Kerr and Lady Hale.

## Omissions

The law makes a distinction between a positive act and an omission. The general rule in negligence is that there is no liability for an omission. In *Donoghue v Stevenson* [1932] Lord Atkin spoke of liability for 'acts and omissions' but he meant omissions in the course of conduct. For example, if a driver is driving towards a bend, omits to brake and as a result crashes into a lamp post, the driver will be liable in negligence. The driver cannot claim it is an omission as it must be seen in relation to the positive act of driving.

A person is not liable for a pure omission which is unrelated to a course of conduct. For example, if you see someone fall into a river and drown you are not liable in negligence for omitting to save them.

Liability in negligence is based on the principle of fault, that someone is only liable if they have done a negligent act. This is seen as worse than merely allowing something to happen.

If the law did impose liability for omissions this would cause a number of problems. It would impose a burden on people to help others. But who would have to help a drowning person, everyone? Or only those who could swim? There would also be difficulties with causation, for example, by not saving someone from drowning have you caused their death?

## Exceptions to the general rule

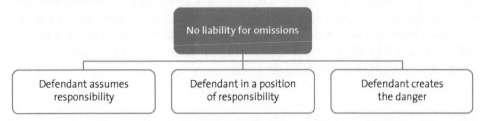

### *The defendant assumes responsibility for the claimant*

If in the circumstances the defendant takes responsibility for the claimant then a duty to act could arise. In *Barrett v Ministry of Defence* [1995] 3 All ER 87 an off-duty pilot at an RAF base in Norway drank himself into a coma on cheap alcohol and collapsed. He was taken to his room but later choked on his vomit and died. The Court of Appeal said that there was no duty to stop an adult drinking alcohol. However, once the defendant found the pilot in a coma they assumed responsibility for him and should have called for medical help. The defendant was negligent but the dead pilot was found to be 25% contributory negligent.

### *The defendant is in a position of responsibility*

If there is an existing relationship where the defendant is in a position of responsibility in relation to the claimant then the defendant will owe a duty of care to act. The following are examples:

❖ parent and child
❖ doctor and patient
❖ captain and passenger
❖ teacher and pupil
❖ lifeguard and swimmer
❖ employer and employee.

### *The defendant creates the danger*

If the defendant creates the danger or makes the situation worse the defendant is under a duty to act to help the claimant. The fire brigade do not owe a duty of care to individual house owners. But if they created the danger or made it worse they would owe a duty. In *Capital & Counties plc v Hampshire County Council* [1997] 2 All ER 865 the defendants attended a fire in a factory. The senior fire officer ordered the sprinkler system to be turned off and as a result the factory burned down. The defendants were liable in negligence because they made the situation worse.

## Liability for the acts of third parties

Following on from the rule that there is no liability for omissions, generally there is no liability for harm caused by a third party. For example, A is not liable for harm to

B caused by a third party C. In *Perl v London Borough of Camden* [1984] QB 342 the defendant owned a block of flats and the claimant rented one for his business. The flat next door was empty and there was no lock on the front door. Burglars went into the empty flat, knocked a hole in the wall and stole clothes from the claimant's business. The Court of Appeal said that although the risk of burglary was foreseeable the defendant had no control over the burglars and was not liable for their actions.

## Exceptions to the general rule

Proximity of claimant and defendant | Proximity of defendant and third party | Defendant creates the danger

### Proximity of claimant and defendant

Whether there is a sufficiently close proximity has to be judged in each case. A contractual relationship may create proximity. In *Stansbie v Troman* [1948] 2 KB 48 the defendant, was left in the claimant's house to decorate it and promised to lock the front door if he went out. He forgot to do so and the claimant was burgled. It was held that the contract between them created proximity and the defendant was liable for the actions of the burglar.

This decision can be distinguished from *Hill v Chief Constable of West Yorkshire* [1988] where there was no proximity between the defendant and the claimant's daughter.

### Proximity of the defendant and the third party

If the defendant has control over the third party this may create a relationship of proximity if it is also foreseeable that the claimant will suffer harm.

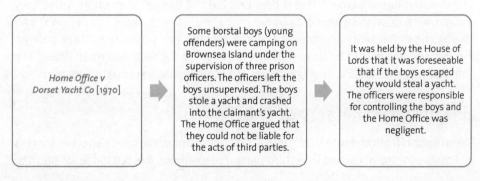

## Defendant creates the danger

If the defendant negligently creates the danger the defendant may be liable if a third party uses that danger to injure the claimant. An example of this is *Haynes v Harwood* [1935] 1 KB 146. The defendant left a horse-drawn van unattended in a busy street and a child threw a stone at the horse, which bolted. The claimant police officer was injured trying to stop the horse. The court said that it was foreseeable someone would try and stop the horse and the defendant was liable for the act of the child.

The courts have distinguished between a normal danger for which there would be no liability and a special danger which does lead to liability. In *Topp v London Country Bus* [1993] 3 All ER 448 the defendant left a mini-bus unlocked with the keys in it at a bus stop between shifts. It was the normal practice at the time to do this. The next driver failed to turn up. A third party stole the mini-bus and knocked down and killed the claimant's wife. The Court of Appeal said that leaving the mini-bus did not create a special danger and the defendant was not liable for the act of the third party. This seems a fine distinction between the unattended horse, which is dangerous and the mini-bus with the keys in, which is not.

# Rescuers

As a general rule there is no liability in negligence for an omission. Consequently there is no general duty to rescue someone in danger.

## Defendant puts claimant in danger

If a defendant puts someone in danger and a rescuer goes to help and is injured, is the defendant liable to the rescuer? If it is foreseeable that someone will go to the rescue then the defendant owes a separate and independent duty to the rescuer. A duty is owed to both amateur and professional rescuers. In *Chadwick v British Railways Board* [1967] 1 WLR 912 a duty was owed to an amateur rescuer who lived near a railway line and went to help after a train crash in which many people were killed. He suffered psychiatric harm and the defendant was found liable in negligence.

## Defendant puts themselves in danger

If the defendant negligently puts themselves in danger the defendant will owe a duty of care to the rescuer as long as the rescuer is not acting in a foolhardy way. In *Baker v Hopkins* [1959] 3 All ER 225 two employees of the defendant were pumping water out of a well and were overcome by carbon monoxide fumes from the pump. The claimant doctor went down the well to help but he too was overcome by the fumes and all three died. The Court of Appeal said that if the employees were in trouble someone would help them so a duty of care was owed to the doctor. The doctor's actions were not foolhardy as he was trying to save lives. Neither had he consented. The defendant was negligent.

## Common Pitfall

Sometimes it is assumed that because a person goes to the rescue and is injured that they have consented to the injury. The courts are reluctant to find that rescuers have consented unless they act in a foolhardy manner.

The United States judge Cardozo CJ once said, 'Danger invites rescue.'

# Public bodies

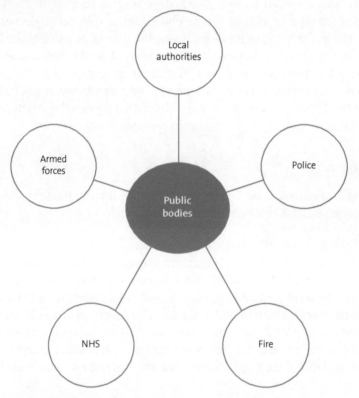

## Local authorities

Whether a public body can be made liable in negligence at common law is a difficult question to answer. There are many sound policy reasons why a public body should not be made liable which include:

❖ Compensation is paid from public funds, which takes resources away from providing services.
❖ It may lead to defensive practices to avoid being found liable.
❖ There may be alternative ways to obtain a remedy, for example, to bring proceedings for judicial review in the High Court against the local authority.

An important fact is that public bodies will be acting under statutory powers. These powers may either give a duty to act (must act) or merely a power to act (may act) and this will be important in determining whether the local authority can be made liable in negligence. It has been argued that a mere power to act means that the local authority does not have to act and so cannot be made liable in negligence.

The courts have made a distinction between *policy matters* which involve the authority deciding how resources are allocated and this involves the exercise of discretion; and *operational matters* which are decisions about how services are carried out.

It has been argued that there is no liability in negligence for policy matters because these decisions were up to the local authority alone. However, there could be liability for operational matters.

The general approach of the courts is that public bodies are not liable in negligence.

### Case precedent – *X v Bedfordshire County Council* [1995] 3 All ER 353

**Facts:** A number of claims were made against the defendant in negligence. Some involved a failure to take children into care and they suffered abuse and some failure to provide for children's special educational needs.

**Principle:** The House of Lords said that although the tests of foreseeability and proximity were met it was not just and reasonable to impose a duty on the defendant. The statutory system to prevent abuse involved a number of different agencies, including local authorities, the police, the education authority etc. and to make one liable would be unjust. To impose a duty on all of them would make it impossible to determine which one was liable. Therefore the defendant was not liable.

**Application:** In applying the rules it is difficult to establish that a public authority is liable in common law negligence for, amongst other reasons, the financial burden this would impose and the complications of overlap with statutory systems.

The claimants then appealed to the European Court of Human Rights. In *Z v UK* (2001) FLR 612 it was found that the defendant had breached Article 3 freedom from inhuman or degrading treatment and the claimants were awarded damages.

*X v Bedfordshire CC* [1995] showed that it is difficult to sue a local authority in negligence for failure to exercise its statutory powers. But the courts later showed that the strict rule against liability could be relaxed. In *W v Essex County Council* [2000] 2 All ER 237 the claimant parents wished to foster a child and told the defendant they did not want anyone who abused children. The defendant placed a 15 year old boy with the claimants. He had abused children, he abused the claimant's children and the claimants suffered psychiatric harm. The House of Lords said that the claimants had an arguable case. The case was later settled out of court.

Even if a claim in negligence fails it may be possible to sue under the Human Rights Act 1998. In *Rabone v Pennine NHS Foundation Trust* [2012] UKSC 2 a young woman committed suicide shortly after being released from a mental hospital. Her parents successfully sued for breach of Article 2, the right to life, under the European Convention on Human Rights.

## The police
In dealing with the police a distinction is also made between operational matters and policy matters.

❖ An operational matter is about how the police carry out their day to day work. The police may be sued in negligence in the normal way. For example, if you are walking along the pavement and a police car knocks you down you may sue for negligence.
❖ A policy matter is about how the police allocate resources.

In *Rigby v Chief Constable of Northamptonshire* [1985] 2 All ER 985 a burglar broke into the claimant's gun shop and started firing guns. The police fired a CS gas canister into the shop which started a fire. The police knew the risk of fire but did not have any firefighting equipment. It was held that the police were liable in negligence.

The leading case is *Hill v Chief Constable of West Yorkshire* [1988] in which the House of Lords said that the police did not owe a duty to individual members of the public and could not be found liable for negligence in the investigation and suppression of crime. This became known as the '*Hill* principle'. However, it is not a blanket ban on suing the police.

The House of Lords applied *Hill* in the following two cases which were heard together, as they involved the common issue of police liability in cases of known threats.

In *Smith v Chief Constable of Sussex* [2008] UKHL 50 Smith told the police that he had received phone calls and text messages from J, his former partner, threatening to kill him. The police did not take any action. Shortly after this J attacked S with a hammer and badly injured him. S sued for negligence. Even though information had been given about a known third party the police were not liable. It was in the public interest that no liability was owed to individuals otherwise it would lead to defensive policing.

In *Van Colle v Chief Constable of Hertfordshire Police* [2008] UKHL 50 VC was a witness against B for a minor theft. Before the trial B made threatening phone calls to VC which VC reported to the police but no action was taken. Just before the trial B shot VC dead and B was convicted of murder. VC's parents sued for breach of Article 2 of the European Convention on Human Rights, the right to life. The court said that for such a claim to succeed it had to be shown that there was a 'real and immediate' risk to the life of an identified person. B had no record of violence and there was no real and immediate risk to VC. The parents' claim failed.

The *Hill* principle was applied more recently in the next case.

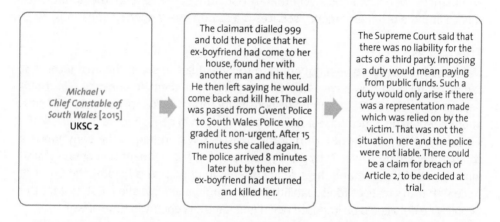

*Michael v Chief Constable of South Wales* [2015] UKSC 2

The claimant dialled 999 and told the police that her ex-boyfriend had come to her house, found her with another man and hit her. He then left saying he would come back and kill her. The call was passed from Gwent Police to South Wales Police who graded it non-urgent. After 15 minutes she called again. The police arrived 8 minutes later but by then her ex-boyfriend had returned and killed her.

The Supreme Court said that there was no liability for the acts of a third party. Imposing a duty would mean paying from public funds. Such a duty would only arise if there was a representation made which was relied on by the victim. That was not the situation here and the police were not liable. There could be a claim for breach of Article 2, to be decided at trial.

In *Michael* dissenting judgments were delivered by Lady Hale and Lord Kerr. They argued that if the police know of an imminent threat of death or injury to a particular person, which they could prevent, then they should owe them a duty of care in negligence.

## The fire and rescue services
The fire service do not owe a duty of care to individuals. There is no common law duty in negligence to attend a fire after receiving a 999 call. The fire service will be liable if they create the danger or make the position worse. In *Capital & Counties plc v Hampshire County Council* [1997] the fire brigade attended a fire in a factory. The fire officer in charge turned off the sprinkler system and as a result the factory burned down. It was held that this was an act no reasonable fire officer would do and the fire brigade were liable in negligence because they had made the position worse.

## The ambulance service

Unlike the police and fire services the ambulance service may owe a duty of care to individual members of the public in certain circumstances.

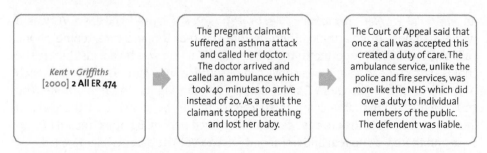

*Kent v Griffiths* [2000] 2 All ER 474

The pregnant claimant suffered an asthma attack and called her doctor. The doctor arrived and called an ambulance which took 40 minutes to arrive instead of 20. As a result the claimant stopped breathing and lost her baby.

The Court of Appeal said that once a call was accepted this created a duty of care. The ambulance service, unlike the police and fire services, was more like the NHS which did owe a duty to individual members of the public. The defendent was liable.

This duty would not arise if the caller was told they would have to wait or that no ambulances were available. Whether this distinction between the ambulance service and the other emergency services is a strong one is open to question.

## The forces

The armed forces will owe a duty of care to individuals in some circumstances, if it can be established they have assumed a duty towards them. In *Barrett v Ministry of Defence* [1995] the MOD assumed responsibility for a drunken pilot. In combat situations it would be difficult to establish a duty. A claim in negligence failed in *Mulcahy v Ministry of Defence* [1996]. During the first Gulf War in Iraq in the early 1990s a commander ordered an artillery gun to be fired while the claimant soldier was standing in front of the gun and the soldier suffered injuries. It was held by the Court of Appeal that the tests of foreseeability and proximity were satisfied. But as a matter of policy no duty could be imposed when engaging the enemy in time of war.

In *Smith v Ministry of Defence* [2013] two claims arose from the second Gulf War in Iraq in 2003. The first claim involved British tanks firing on other British tanks. It was argued that this was negligence for not fitting equipment to enable tanks to recognise other British tanks. The second claim involved soldiers in Land Rovers killed by roadside bombs: was this a breach of Article 2? The Supreme Court said that the decision about equipment in tanks was made well before military action and the MOD could not claim 'combat immunity'. As regards the Land Rovers, decisions made at a high level in the MOD or on the battlefield would not be a breach of Article 2 but a claim for something in between these two could be successful.

# Putting it into practice

Read the question below and attempt an outline answer.

Explain the requirements to establish a duty of care in negligence and discuss how they are used to control the scope of the duty.

# Outline answer – development of negligence, *Caparo* test, policy factors

❖ This essay will examine the tests from *Caparo* which are used to determine whether a duty of care is owed and it will consider how the courts have used those tests in the context of the law of negligence.

❖ The modern law of negligence has developed from the decision in *Donoghue v Stevenson* and the statement by Lord Atkin that we owe a duty to our neighbours, who are those people we ought to have in mind when contemplating the act we are doing.

    ❖ This became known as the neighbour principle and this general principle enabled the tort of negligence to expand. In *Anns v Merton London Borough Council* Lord Wilberforce set out a two-stage test for duty, that we should assume there is a duty unless there is a good reason why there should not be.

    ❖ This expansion continued during the 1970s but in *Caparo v Dickman* the House of Lords said that negligence should develop incrementally and set out a three-stage test for establishing a duty of foreseeability, proximity and just and reasonableness.

❖ The test of foreseeability is would the reasonable person in the defendant's position foresee that the claimant would suffer harm if the defendant did a particular act. This can be shown in *Bourhill v Young* where it was held that it was not foreseeable that someone 15 metres away and out of sight of the accident would suffer shock.

❖ The requirement of proximity is that there is a close relationship between the claimant and the defendant. The degree of closeness depends in part on the type of harm suffered, for example, claims for physical injury need less closeness than for financial damage. In *Watson v BBBC* it was held that there was proximity between the parties because boxers relied on the BBBC to have sound rules.

❖ The third requirement was applied in *Hill v Chief Constable of West Yorkshire* where the court held it would not be just and reasonable to impose liability because of the number of potential victims.

❖ These three requirements also relate to one another, for example, if there is proximity it is more likely to be just and reasonable that a duty exists.

    ❖ The courts have used the three requirements of the *Caparo* test in a flexible way. Often policy reasons will influence decisions even though they are not made explicit. In *Bourhill* the court focused on foreseeability but equally it could have relied on policy that damages should not be given for psychiatric harm.

    ❖ Policy arguments may also be used to distinguish where a duty may or may not be owed. In *Kent v Griffiths* [2000] the court rejected the policy arguments used to prevent the police and fire service being liable and made the ambulance service liable because it was part of the health service.

❖ In *Michael v Chief Constable of South Wales Police* Lord Toulson said that proximity and fairness could not be sufficiently defined to make them practical tests. All three are rather vague concepts and how they are interpreted by judges will vary. A court may say that something is not foreseeable or that there is no proximity. However, if these principles are seen in the wider context of the purpose of the duty of care to restrict liability in negligence the fact they are open to interpretation doesn't matter as long as they are used to reach just decisions.

## Table of key cases referred to in this chapter

| Key case | Area of law | Principle |
|---|---|---|
| *Caparo v Dickman* [1990] 1 All ER 568 | Liability for negligent mis-statement; and for creating the universal test for the duty of care in negligence. | The test for establishing a duty is foreseeability, proximity, fair, just and reasonableness. |
| *Donoghue v Stevenson* [1932] AC 562 | A friend bought the claimant a bottle of ginger beer in a café. After drinking it the claimant became ill because it had a snail in it. She sued the manufacturer for negligence. | This established the neighbour principle. A person is liable in negligence for harm caused by their actions to anyone it can be foreseen will be injured. |
| *Haynes v Harwood* [1935] 1 KB 146 | The claimant police officer was injured stopping a runaway horse which had been left untethered, in a busy street by the defendant. | A duty is owed to a foreseeable rescuer. The defendant was liable in negligence to the police officer. |
| *Hill v Chief Constable of West Yorkshire* [1988] 2 All ER 238 | The claimant sued the police for negligence for not arresting a murderer sooner. He had killed 13 women including the claimant's daughter. The House of Lords held the police were not liable. | In the investigation and suppression of crime the police were not liable in negligence. No duty is owed to individual members of the public. Known as the *Hill* principle. |
| *Home Office v Dorset Yacht Co* [1970] AC 1004 | Borstal boys escaped, stole a yacht and crashed into the claimant's yacht. | House of Lords said that the Home Office had control of the boys and were negligent. This is an exception to the general rule that you are not liable for the acts of a third party. |

| *Kent v Griffiths* [2000] 2 All ER 274 | Claim against the ambulance service for negligence for being late and causing harm to the claimant. | The Court of Appeal said that the ambulance service was like the NHS and once a call was accepted it did owe a duty to individual members of the public. |
|---|---|---|
| *Michael v Chief Constable of South Wales Police* [2015] UKSC 2 | Claim against police for negligence for being late to a call and not stopping a murder. | The Supreme Court applied the *Hill* principle and said the police were not liable. |
| *X v Bedfordshire County Council* [1995] 3 All ER 353 | Claims against the council for negligence in respect of child abuse. | It is not fair, just and reasonable to make the council liable as there is a statutory system to prevent abuse. |

---

@ **Visit the book's companion website to test your knowledge**

❖ Resources include a subject map, revision tip podcasts, downloadable diagrams, MCQ quizzes for each chapter and a flashcard glossary

❖ www.routledge.com/cw/optimizelawrevision

# 2 Negligence: Breach of Duty

## Revision objectives

**Understand the law**
- Can you explain the test applied to determine if a defendant has breached their duty of care?
- Can you identify the four factors relevant to setting the standard of care?
- Can you outline the test applied to determine if someone with a skill has acted negligently?
- Can you identify the three requirements to establish *res ipsa loquitur*?

**Remember the details**
- Can you explain the two factors of likelihood of injury and risk of serious injury?
- Can you explain the relevance of the Compensation Act 2006 s1 to the standard of care?
- Can you explain, using cases, the standard of care expected of children?
- Can you explain how acting in an emergency affects the liability of the defendant?
- Can you explain the effect of establishing *res ipsa loquitur*?

**Reflect critically on areas of debate**
- Can you explain and distinguish the cases on illness and the standard of care?
- Can you explain the liability of drivers of emergency vehicles responding to a call?

**Contextualise**
- Do you understand the possible relationships between the four factors used to determine the standard of care?
- Do you understand the circumstances when the normal standard of care does not apply?

**Apply your skills and knowledge**
- Can you answer the question at the end of this chapter?

# Chapter Map

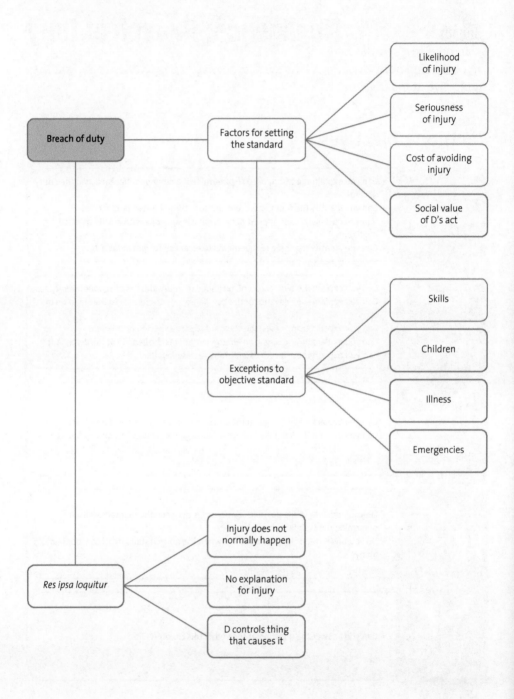

# The standard of the reasonable person

Once a duty of care has been established the second question to ask is whether the defendant is in breach of that duty. In deciding this, the courts look at the defendant's conduct which is judged by the standard of a reasonable person. This is an objective standard which means the defendant's actions are looked at from an outside point of view, the objective observer. This is the opposite to applying a subjective standard and looking at it from the defendant's point of view. If the defendant does not reach the standard of a reasonable person in carrying out the particular act then the defendant is negligent. The reasonable person is a hypothetical person which enables the courts to set the standard required.

Traditionally the cases have referred to the 'reasonable man' but in modern times it is more appropriate to talk about the reasonable person. Judges have often referred to the reasonable man as 'the man on the Clapham omnibus'. This is not the average person. The standard was set out by Baron Alderson in *Blyth v Birmingham Waterworks* [1856] 11 Exch 781:

> 'Negligence is the omission to do something which a reasonable man would do or doing something which a prudent and reasonable man would not do.'

The standard was explained by Lord Macmillan in *Glasgow Corporation v Muir* [1943] AC 448:

> 'It eliminates the personal equation and is independent of the idiosyncrasies of the particular person whose conduct is in question.'

The 'reasonable person' is not the perfect person, nor the average person. It is a person who will usually act in a reasonable way. It is the judge in each case who determines this standard.

# Factors relevant to setting the standard

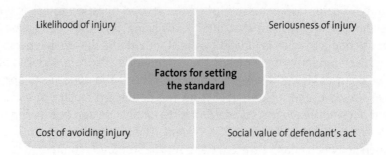

In determining whether the defendant is in breach of duty the courts take a number of factors into consideration. The factors set out below are not exclusive and other relevant factors can be taken into account.

The factors have to be considered both individually and in relation to each other. For example, if it is easy to avoid injury and the act has little social value that would lead to a conclusion there is a breach of duty. In *The Wagon Mound (No 1)* [1961] AC 388 when oil was discharged into Sydney harbour, this could easily have been prevented and it was not a benefit to anyone.

## Likelihood of injury
The more likely it is that an injury will occur the higher the standard expected of the defendant.

### Case precedent – *Bolton v Stone* [1951] AC 850

**Facts:** Miss Stone was standing in the street when she was hit by a cricket ball from the defendant's cricket ground. The ball had been hit nearly 100 metres over a three metre high fence. Cricket balls had only been hit outside the ground six times in 30 years.

**Principle:** The House of Lords held that it was foreseeable that someone outside the ground would be hit. However, the likelihood of injury was extremely small and the defendants were not in breach of their duty. The reasonable man 'would have done nothing' according to Lord Radcliffe.

**Application:** If the risk is low then no action need be taken but if the risk of harm is high it is more likely that precautions should be taken. The other factors are also relevant in determining this. For example playing cricket is socially useful.

If people were trying to break bottles by throwing stones at them and the claimant was hit by a stone would this lead to a different conclusion?

## The seriousness of injury

If there is a risk of serious injury then a higher standard of care is expected of the defendant. This may be the case even if the risk of harm happening is low. This is shown in *Paris v Stepney Borough Council* [1951] AC 367. The claimant was blind in one eye. He worked at the defendant's garage and was scraping rust off the bottom of a bus when a splinter of metal went into his good eye and blinded him. He had not been given goggles which was the normal practice. The House of Lords said that even though the risk of injury was small his disability increased the risk of serious injury because it meant he could be made blind. Therefore the defendant was liable.

## The cost of avoiding the injury

What measures should the defendant take to avoid the harm happening? The costs of avoiding the harm must be balanced against the harm which could happen. In *Bolton v Stone* [1951] should the cricket club have built a five metres high fence or built a roof over the ground or stopped playing cricket? Each of these solutions has to be balanced against the low risk of harm.

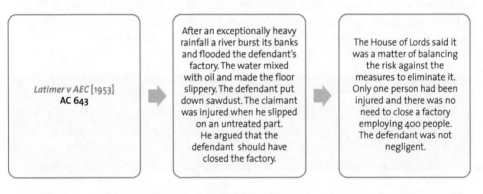

*Latimer v AEC* [1953] **AC 643**

After an exceptionally heavy rainfall a river burst its banks and flooded the defendant's factory. The water mixed with oil and made the floor slippery. The defendant put down sawdust. The claimant was injured when he slipped on an untreated part. He argued that the defendant should have closed the factory.

The House of Lords said it was a matter of balancing the risk against the measures to eliminate it. Only one person had been injured and there was no need to close a factory employing 400 people. The defendant was not negligent.

## The social value of the defendant's action

If the defendant is doing an act which is a benefit to society, the courts will balance this against the risk the defendant is taking. In *Watt v Herts County Council* [1954] 1 WLR 835 a woman was trapped under a car after a road accident. A heavy jack was needed to lift the car and free the woman. The fire brigade used an unsuitable lorry to transport the jack, it slipped and injured the claimant fire officer and he sued for negligence. There was a ten minute wait for a suitable lorry. The Court of Appeal held that the defendants did owe a duty of care to the claimant. But the defendants were trying to save a life and they had fulfilled their duty.

> 'If this accident had occurred in a commercial enterprise without any emergency there could be no doubt that the servant would succeed. But the commercial end to make a profit is very different from the human end to save life or limb.'
>
> Denning LJ.

## Aim Higher

Read *Watt v Herts County Council* [1954] and the judgment of Denning LJ.

Explain what he said about balancing the risks and emergency vehicles stopping at red lights.

Also read 'Sound the Alarm' by Karen O'Sullivan, 2015, 165 NLJ 7678 p and 10 for the modern view on emergency vehicles.

The significance of the social usefulness factor was highlighted by concerns over the 'compensation culture'. This is a belief that people are suing when they suffer an injury whatever the circumstances and this may stop others carrying out socially useful activities in case someone is injured. The Compensation Act 2006 s1 provides that in considering the standard of care in negligence and what steps the defendant should have taken, courts may take into account whether requiring the defendant to take such steps would prevent a desirable activity or discourage a desirable activity. For example, schools taking pupils on school trips.

## Common Pitfall

The above four factors are sometimes left out when answering problem questions or all of them are put in whether they are relevant or not. The best approach is to select those factors which are relevant to the facts and apply them.

## Exceptions to the objective standard

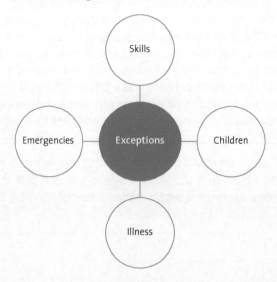

## Skills

If the defendant has a particular skill they are not judged by the standard of the reasonable person who does not have that skill. They are judged by a different standard, the *Bolam* test.

> **Case precedent – *Bolam v Frien Hospital Management Committee* [1957] 2 All ER 118**
>
> **Facts:** B suffered from depression and agreed to a course of electro-convulsive therapy. There were three different views amongst doctors to give relaxant drugs or physically restrain the patient or neither. B was not given drugs or restrained. During treatment he fell off the bed and was injured.
>
> **Principle:** It was held that the defendant doctor had acted in accordance with a competent body of medical opinion and was found not negligent.
>
> **Application:** This principle has been applied to a wide range of jobs and activities which require a skill from being a pilot to playing football.

In *Bolam* McNair J said, 'A man need not possess the highest expert skill; it is well established law that it is sufficient if he exercises the ordinary skill of an ordinary competent man exercising that particular art.'

The House of Lords put a qualification on the *Bolam* principle in *Bolitho v City and Hackney Health Authority* [1997] 4 All ER 771. They said that before a court accepted a medical opinion as responsible the court had to be satisfied that doctors had considered the risks and benefits of the proposed treatment and had reached a 'defensible' conclusion. The effect of this decision is that a court will not simply accept what a responsible body of medical opinion says but will consider whether it has a logical basis.

If someone carries out a skilled task but lacks the skill or experience to reach the required standard they will be in breach of their duty of care. In *Nettleship v Weston* [1971] 3 All ER 581 the defendant asked the claimant, who was a family friend, to teach her to drive. On the third lesson the defendant suddenly drove the car on to the pavement and hit a lamp post injuring the claimant. What standard did the defendant have to reach? Was it the standard of a learner driver? The court said that she had to reach the standard of the competent experienced driver and as she had not done so she was liable in negligence.

Although this may seem a harsh decision because the law imposes a high standard, it is trying to protect people. If someone drives a car they must reach the above standard and they can reach this standard through supervision. A doctor has a duty to tell the patient of any material risks of treatment and any reasonable alternatives.

A material risk is one which a person in the patient's position would see as significant (prudent patient test) *Montgomery v Lanarkshire Health Board* [2015] UKSC 11.

## Children

Children cannot be expected to reach the standard of care required of adults as they lack the knowledge and experience of adults. The standard applied to children is the standard of a reasonable child of that age.

*Mullin v Richards* [1998] **1 All ER 920** ➡ Two 15 year old schoolgirls were friends. During a lesson they were having a sword fight with plastic rulers. One of the rulers snapped and a piece of plastic went in the claimant's eye and blinded her. The High Court ruled that the defendant was negligent, although the claimant was 50% contributorily negligent. ➡ The Court of Appeal said that the test of foreseeability was whether a reasonable child of the same age would foresee the risk. There was no evidence that plastic rulers broke easily and the school had not banned playing with them. The defendant had not been negligent.

In *Orchard v Lee* [2009] EWCA Civ 295 a 13 year old schoolboy was playing tag in the playground at lunch time. He ran into a supervisor and injured her. The Court of Appeal said that the boy was playing the game in the normal way and not breaking any rules. For a child to be negligent they had to act with a 'very high degree' of carelessness. The boy was not negligent. More recently in *Jackson v Murray* [2015] UKSC 5 the Supreme Court considered the liability of a 13 year old schoolgirl who was knocked down by a car as she was crossing the road from behind a school mini-bus. She was found as equally to blame as the driver.

## Illness

If the claimant has an illness or disability and the defendant knows this or ought to foresee it, the defendant will owe a higher standard of care. In *Haley v London Electricity Board* [1964] 3 All ER 185 a blind man fell into a trench which the defendants had dug in the street in London. A pickaxe handle had been put across the front of the trench which would have been a sufficient warning for someone with normal sight. The House of Lords held that given the number of blind people in London the defendants ought to have realised the risk to blind people and they were negligent.

If the defendant has an illness but does not realise, this is taken into account in determining if the defendant is in breach of a duty of care. In *Roberts v Ramsbottom* [1980] 1 All ER 7 a 73 year old driver collided with the claimant's parked car and injured her. The defendant argued that he had had a stroke 20 minutes before the accident but did not realise and was not negligent. Just before the accident he had been in two other minor collisions and had admitted that he felt strange. The court said that he had continued to drive even though he should have realised he was ill. He was therefore negligent.

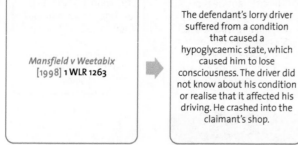

The above cases seem to be contradictory. However, in *Roberts* the defendant admitted to feeling strange and the court therefore found that he was negligent in continuing to drive.

In *Dunnage v Randall* [2015] EWCA Civ 673 the defendant who suffered from paranoid schizophrenia, a mental disorder, set fire to himself with petrol and died from his burns. The claimant, his nephew, tried to stop him and suffered serious burns. He sued the defendant's estate for negligence. In the county court it was held that the defendant's action was not voluntary, he did not realise what he was doing because of his mental illness and he did not owe a duty of care to the claimant. The Court of Appeal said that the defendant had to meet the objective standard. He still had physical control of his actions, he did owe a duty to the claimant and was in breach of that duty therefore the estate was liable. *Dunnage* also contradicts *Mansfield v Weetabix* and seems to ignore the defendant's condition and effectively makes them strictly liable.

## Emergencies

If the defendant is acting in an emergency this is taken into account in deciding what standard they have to reach. The law accepts a lower standard from the defendant. For example, if someone stops to give first aid at a road accident the fact that it is an emergency is taken into account. In *Marshall v Osmond* [1983] 2 All ER 225 a police car was chasing suspects in another car and skidded into it, injuring the claimant. This happened at night while driving on gravel. It was held that the police do owe a duty to someone they are chasing but in these circumstances the police had fulfilled that duty.

## *Res ipsa loquitur*

In a claim for negligence the burden is on the claimant to prove that the defendant is in breach of the duty of care. However, in some circumstances it is clear that the defendant has acted negligently. All three requirements set out below must be met for the rule to apply. *Res ipsa loquitur* means, 'the thing speaks for itself'. This rule was originally set out in the following case.

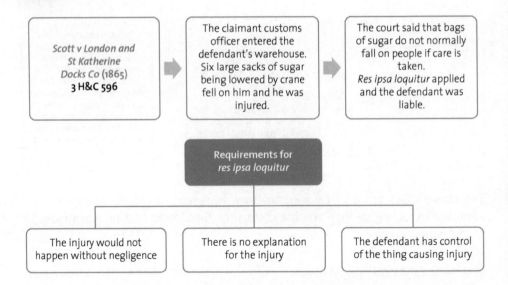

## The injury would not normally happen without negligence

These are situations in which it is obvious that the defendant has acted negligently, for example, items being left in patients during operations or a patient having the wrong limb amputated. In *Mahon v Osborne* [1939] 2 KB 14 the claimant had an operation on their abdomen. It was later found that a swab (a cotton wool pad) had been left in their body and as a result the patient died. The defendant surgeon was unable to explain this. It was held that *res ipsa loquitur* applied and he was liable in negligence.

## There is no explanation for the accident

If there is evidence of how the accident happened then it is up to the claimant to prove negligence in the normal way. If there is no evidence of how the accident happened then *res ipsa loquitur* will apply.

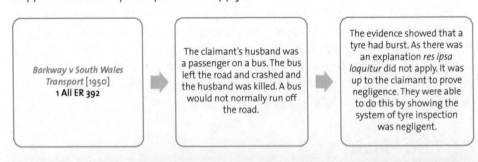

## Common Pitfall

If a problem question gives a reason why an accident has happened then *res ipsa loquitur* does not apply.

## The defendant must have control of the thing which causes the harm

This can be illustrated by the following two cases. In *Gee v Metropolitan Railway Co* (1873) LR 8 QB 161 a train had recently left the station. The claimant leaned against a door, fell out and was injured. It was held that the defendant had control of the train and the door and *res ipsa loquitur* applied. In contrast in *Easson v London and North Eastern Railway Co* [1944] KB 421 a train had travelled seven miles from a station. The claimant, aged four, fell out of a door of the train. It was held that the defendant did not have control of the train as any passenger going along the corridor could have opened the door. *Res ipsa loquitur* did not apply.

### The effect of *res ipsa loquitur*

It has been argued that the effect of *res ipsa loquitur* is to reverse the burden of proof. If the claimant shows that *res ipsa loquitur* applies it is up to the defendant to prove that the defendant was not negligent. In *Ward v Tesco* [1976] 1 All ER 219 the claimant slipped on some yoghurt which had been spilt on the floor of one of the defendant's shops. The Court of Appeal said that the claimant would not have slipped if the floor was clean and *res ipsa loquitur* applied. It was up to the defendant to show that they were not negligent. They gave evidence of their cleaning procedures but this was not sufficient and they were found negligent.

The courts have turned against the idea that *res ipsa loquitur* reverses the burden of proof. In *Ng Chun Pui v Lee Chuen Tat* [1988] RTR 298 in the Privy Council Lord Griffiths stated:

> 'it is misleading to talk of the burden of proof shifting to the defendant in a *res ipsa loquitur* situation. The burden of proving negligence rests throughout the case on the claimant.'

## Putting it into practice

Read the question below and attempt an outline answer.

Alice's partner Bob worked late shifts in a factory. One Saturday night he came home from work early about 11.00 pm and found her in bed having sex with one of his friends. His friend ran out of the house. Bob slapped Alice hard in the face causing her a black eye. He told her he was going to the pub and that when he came back he would beat her up. Bob then left the house. Alice was so frightened she phoned '999' and asked for Wessex Police and told the operator what had happened. The operator told her to stay in the house and he would send police officers to see her. The police were very busy that night. Police officers did not arrive at Alice's house until an hour after her call by which time Bob had come back and beaten her up.

Carol, a 14 year old school girl, was playing rugby for her school against their local rivals. Carol jumped up to catch the ball at the same time as Daisy, an opposition player. Carol's elbow caught Daisy in the face and knocked out two of her teeth.

Eve is a diabetic and needs to take medication each day and to eat regularly to keep her glucose levels up. One day she had been very busy. She was driving to school to pick up her daughter when she fainted due to lack of glucose in her bloodstream. Her car went on to the pavement and knocked down and injured Fatima.

**Advise Alice, Daisy and Fatima of the claims they may make, if any, in negligence.**

## Outline answer – negligence, duty of care and breach of duty

This question involves issues of whether a duty of care exists and if there is a breach of duty in the case of the police, a child and someone driving with a medical condition; it also involves acts of third parties.

❖  *Alice v Wessex Police*
   - ❖  Alice needs to show that the police owe her a duty of care, they have broken that duty and caused her harm.
   - ❖  Duty, *Hill v Chief Constable of West Yorkshire* 2 All ER 238 held that the police do not owe a duty to individual members of the public as regards the investigation and suppression of crime. It is a Saturday and the police are busy – should they have sent officers quicker? In *Michael* the court said that the police did not assume responsibility; Alice's situation could be distinguished from *Michael* as they said they would send officers and also advised her to stay in the house.
   - ❖  The other issue is third parties; in both *Smith v Chief Constable of Sussex* [2008] UKHL 50 and *Michael v Chief Constable of South Wales Police* [2015] UKSC 2 the court held that the police were not liable even when information was given about a known third party; here Alice has told the police of the threat from Bob.
   - ❖  It could be argued that if Lord Kerr's dissenting judgment in *Michael* was followed, there is proximity and a duty would be owed.
   - ❖  If a duty is established are the police in breach of duty? They must reach the standard of a competent skilled police officer. Would such an officer have gone to Alice's house sooner? It is unlikely the courts would wish to be involved in deciding how calls are allocated and the police would not be in breach of duty.

❖ *Daisy v Carol*

   ❖ Daisy needs to show that Carol owes a duty of care to her; the *Caparo* test applies, foreseeability, proximity and fair, just and reasonableness. It is foreseeable that if Carol acts carelessly Daisy would be injured; test of a child of that age, *Mullin v Richards*. Proximity can be shown as there is physical closeness and a relationship as they are both playing on the same pitch. It would also be just and reasonable to owe a duty because the players would be insured by their schools.

   ❖ In *Orchard v Lee* a 13 year old school boy playing tag who ran into a supervisor was not acting negligently because he was playing the game in the normal way. Carol will owe Daisy a duty of care but similarly Carol is acting within the rules and even though it is a rival school there is no evidence Carol has acted deliberately. She is not in breach of duty.

❖ *Fatima v Eve*

   ❖ Does Eve owe a duty of care to Fatima? It is an established duty that a driver owes a duty to other road users. Is Eve in breach of duty? She has to reach the standard of the competent motorist, *Nettleship v Weston*. Would a competent motorist drive in Eve's position? What effect does Eve's medical condition have on her duty? Eve knows of her medical condition but is she at fault for not taking her tablets or not eating. The question does not say. If she has not looked after herself because she has been too busy it may be argued that she is at fault and should not have been driving, *Roberts v Ramsbottom*. However, even if the lack of glucose was not Eve's fault, following *Dunnage v Randall* she would still have to meet the objective standard of a competent driver and would be liable.

# Table of key cases referred to in this chapter

| Key case | Area of law | Principle |
|---|---|---|
| *Bolam v Frien HMC* [1957] 2 All ER 118 | The standard of care expected of a doctor or someone with a skill is higher than the standard of the reasonable person. | A person with a skill is judged by the standard of a competent experienced person with that skill. |
| *Bolton v Stone* [1951] AC 850 | Likelihood of injury is one factor for determining if there is a breach of duty. Cricket balls hit out of ground only six times in 30 years. | If likelihood of injury is low then it is more likely not to be a breach of duty. |

| Key case | Area of law | Principle |
|---|---|---|
| *Dunnage v Randall* [2015] EWCA Civ 673 | A defendant, who suffered from a mental disorder, set himself on fire and injured the claimant. | Someone with a mental disorder who has physical control of his actions has to meet the objective standard of the reasonable person. |
| *Mansfield v Weetabix* [1998] 1 WLR 1263 | A lorry driver had an illness which he did not know about and it affected his driving. He was not liable in negligence. | If someone has an illness they do not know about this is not negligent because they are not at fault. Montgomery v Lanarkshire Health Board [2015] UKSC 11 Doctor's duty to tell of risks of treatment and alternative treatments. No longer the Bolam test but the reasonable person in the patient's position. |
| *Mullin v Richards* [1998] 1 All ER 920 | The standard expected of a 15 year old was that of the ordinary reasonable 15 year old. | A child is judged by a reasonable child of that age. |
| *Nettleship v Weston* [1971] 3 All ER 581 | A learner driver crashed on the third lesson and was in breach of their duty of care. | A learner driver must reach the standard of a competent and experienced driver. |
| *Scott v London and St Katherine Docks* (1865) 3 H&C 596 | Bags of sugar fell on the claimant. This was obviously negligent. | The principle of *res ipsa loquitur* applies and the defendant will be negligent. |

@ Visit the book's companion website to test your knowledge

❖ Resources include a subject map, revision tip podcasts, downloadable diagrams, MCQ quizzes for each chapter and a flashcard glossary

❖ www.routledge.com/cw/optimizelawrevision

# 3

# Negligence: Causation

## Revision objectives

**Understand the law**
- Can you explain the but for test and the test of material contribution?
- Can you explain the general rule on liability for the acts of third parties?
- Can you explain the test to establish legal causation?
- Can you explain what is meant by a new intervening act?
- Can you explain the eggshell skull rule?

**Remember the details**
- Can you explain *Fairchild v Glenhaven Funeral Services* and the effect of that decision?
- Can you explain the legal position of the defendant where there are two consecutive causes of harm?
- Can you explain the legal effect of a new intervening act by the claimant and by a third party using cases to illustrate your answer?
- Can you explain the rule that the kind of damage must be foreseeable to establish legal causation?

**Reflect critically on areas of debate**
- Can you explain how the test of material contribution is applied by the courts?
- Can you explain whether compensation may be given for loss of a chance?

**Contextualise**
- Do you understand that cases in tort have to be proved on a balance of probabilities and how this can be established?
- Do you understand that policy is also a factor in courts making decisions on causation?

**Apply your skills and knowledge**
- Can you answer the question at the end of this chapter?

# Chapter Map

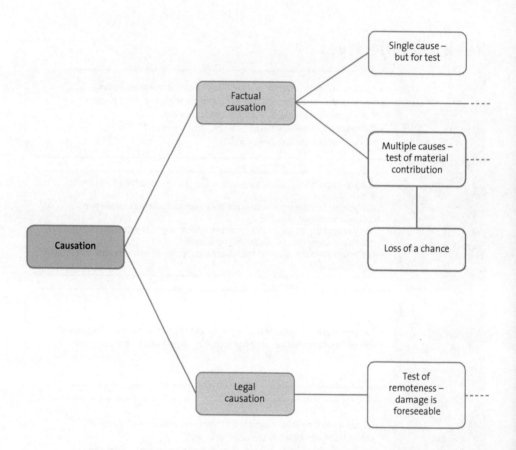

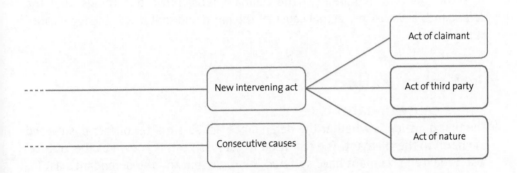

| | New intervening act | | Act of claimant |
|---|---|---|---|
| | | | Act of third party |
| | Consecutive causes | | Act of nature |

Exception eggshell
skull rule –
damage is not
foreseeable

# Introduction

To successfully establish negligence the claimant has to prove three things:

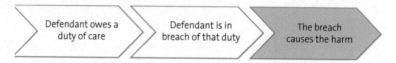

To show this third requirement the claimant must prove two things, that the defendant's act was the factual cause of the harm and that it was the legal cause of the harm.

# Factual causation

## Single cause of harm

The first question is whether the defendant's act as a matter of fact has caused the harm to the claimant. The test used to establish this is known as the 'but for' test. Would the claimant have suffered the harm 'but for' the defendant's act (or except for the defendant's act)?

The answer to this question must be 'no' in order to satisfy the test. If the answer is, no that the claimant would not have suffered harm 'but for' the defendant's act then logically the defendant's act must have caused the harm.

The test can be illustrated by the next case.

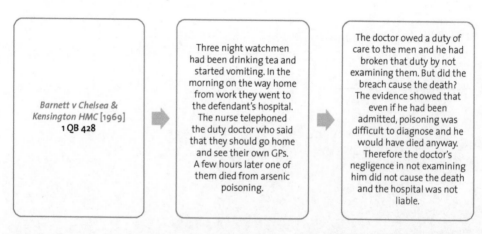

Would the man have died 'but for' the doctor's negligence? The answer was 'yes' because even if he had been admitted to the hospital he would have died anyway. The above case is an example of the 'but for' test giving a clear result. There are some circumstances when the facts are more complex and the 'but for' test is not suitable.

# Multiple causes of harm

If there are two or more causes of the claimant's loss the 'but for' test does not work. A famous example is set out below.

X and Y carelessly start separate fires which spread and at the same time burn down Z's house. If the 'but for' test is used:

❖ Would Z's house have burned down but for X's careless act? The answer is 'yes' because the fire started by Y would have burned down the house. Therefore X would not be liable in negligence.

❖ Would Z's house have burned down but for Y's careless act? The answer is 'yes' because the fire started by X would have burned down the house. Therefore Y is not liable in negligence.

❖ The result is that neither X nor Y would be liable in negligence. This is clearly an unjust result.

One alternative test developed by the courts is the test of 'material contribution'. In *Bonnington Castings v Wardlaw* [1956] AC 613 the claimant developed a lung disease from dust while working in the defendant's factory. Some of the dust was from pneumatic hammers and this dust could not be prevented. Some of the dust came from grinders but they had not been maintained properly and this dust could have been prevented. It was impossible to determine which dust caused the lung disease. The court asked the question whether the dust from the grinders had made a 'material contribution' to the disease and concluded that it had. Therefore the defendant was negligent. The court said that anything other than a minimal amount would be a material contribution.

The Privy Council have said that the causes do not have to be concurrent and can be consecutive.

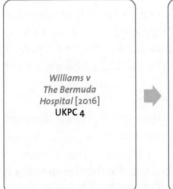

*Williams v The Bermuda Hospital* [2016] **UKPC 4**

➡ The claimant went to the emergency department of the defendant's hospital at 11.17 am and was examined by a doctor at 11.40 am. He was diagnosed with appendicitis but was not operated on until 9.30 pm. It was then found that his appendix had burst and as a result he suffered complications to his heart and lungs. He sued for negligence because of the delay.

➡ At first instance the court said that he could not prove causation because he could not show that if he had been treated within a reasonable time he would have avoided complications. The Privy Council said that a claimant can show a causal link between the breach and the damage by showing the breach materially contributed to the damage. He could show this and was given damages for suffering the complications.

The Privy Council also said that the claimant has to show on a balance of probabilities that the breach materially contributed to the damage. The test of material contribution can be used if two factors cumulatively cause harm. This applies whether the factors operate concurrently or successively.

If the defendant's act materially increased the risk of harm the test of material contribution can also be used.

---

**Case precedent – *McGhee v National Coal Board* [1972] 3 All ER 1008**

**Facts:** The claimant worked in a brick works and developed dermatitis, a skin disease, from the brick dust. He was exposed to brick dust while he was working and this could not be prevented but he had to cycle home covered in brick dust because no showers were provided. Using the 'but for' test the claimant could not prove that the dermatitis was caused by the brick dust on him on the way home because it could have been caused by the brick dust during the day.

**Principle:** The court said that by not providing showers the defendant had 'materially increased' the risk of dermatitis and was therefore negligent.

**Application:** A policy reason behind the decision is that even though the claimant cannot prove his case because the lack of washing facilities increased the risk of dermatitis the employer should be liable. The test of material contribution will be used where there are two or more causes of harm.

---

A further problem with causation arises if instead of two or more causes there are two or more people who could have caused the harm. In these circumstances the courts also use the test of material contribution. In *Fairchild v Glenhaven Funeral Services Ltd* [2002] UKHL 22 the claimants while working for a number of different employers were exposed to asbestos dust and as a result developed mesothelioma. It is possible that the disease could be caused by a single fibre of asbestos and it was impossible for the claimants to prove which employer was responsible. The 'but for' test could not provide an answer. The House of Lords held that by exposing the claimants to the risk of mesothelioma each employer made a material contribution to them contracting the disease. All the employers were liable.

The liability of the employers was 'joint and several' which means that a claimant can sue all the employers or just one for all the damage caused.

In *Fairchild* the courts are trying to balance two competing claims. This is really a matter of policy as to which claim is given precedence in trying to achieve justice.

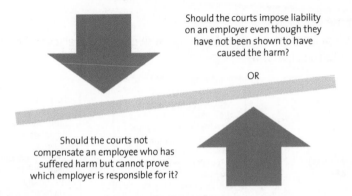

Should the courts impose liability on an employer even though they have not been shown to have caused the harm?

OR

Should the courts not compensate an employee who has suffered harm but cannot prove which employer is responsible for it?

The rule that all the employers were jointly and severally liable was amended in the following later case. In *Barker v Corus UK Ltd* [2006] All ER (D) 23 the claimant had worked for himself, the defendant and another employer which became insolvent. In all three jobs he was exposed to asbestos and developed mesothelioma. The House of Lords said that if more than one person is responsible, liability should be divided in proportion to the time spent with each employer. This meant that each employer was only liable for a proportion and this was just several liability and not joint liability. The effect on the claimant was that the defendant was only liable for the time he spent working for the defendant.

The **Compensation Act 2006** s3 reversed the effect of *Barker*. Under s3(1) if a person has negligently exposed someone to asbestos and as a result the victim has contracted mesothelioma and it is not possible to tell if that exposure or some other exposure caused the victim to become ill, a person is liable in tort. Under s3(2) if others have also exposed the victim to asbestos then liability is joint and several.

In *Heneghan v Manchester Dry Docks Ltd* [2016] EWCA Civ 86 a son sued for damages for his father contracting lung cancer from asbestos and for his premature death. Six employers were responsible for approximately 35% of the deceased's exposure to asbestos. Each had materially contributed to the cancer. The question was whether each employer was jointly and severally liable or only for a proportion? The Court of Appeal applied *Barker* and said that lung cancer and mesothelioma were legally the same and it extended the *Fairchild* rule to lung cancer. The employers were only liable for their individual proportions.

## Up for Debate

The area of causation in tort is a complex one. It will often be part of a problem question on negligence or it may be the topic of an essay question. Read the following article, 'A Material Contribution to Forensic Clarity' by Charles Foster, 2016, 166 NLJ 7689 p9, which explains the law in the light of *Williams v Bermuda Hospitals Board* [2016] UKPC 4.

## Consecutive causes

What is the legal position if after the original negligent act a second negligent act causes harm to the claimant?

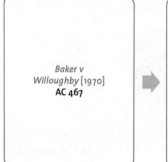

| | | |
|---|---|---|
| *Baker v Willoughby* [1970] **AC 467** | The defendant driver negligently knocked down the claimant, a pedestrian, and injured his leg. Three years later, the claimant was shot in the same leg during a robbery at work. His leg had to be amputated. What was the effect of the second injury? The defendant argued that he was only liable for the loss up to the date of the robbery. | The House of Lords said that a person is compensated for the loss he suffers not the injury. After the road accident the claimant was not able to earn as much as he did before the accident, nor to lead a full life. The second injury did not make the claimant's position worse. The defendant was liable for the full extent of the injuries for the remainder of the claimant's life. |

The legal position is different if after the original negligent act the claimant contracts an unrelated illness. *Jobling v Associated Dairies* [1982] AC 794 in 1973 due to the defendant's negligence the claimant slipped over at work and injured his back. As a result his earning power was reduced. In 1976 before the case came to trial the claimant developed an unrelated disease of the spine which left him unable to work. The High Court awarded him damages for the remainder of his life. The House of Lords said that the aim of damages in tort was to put the claimant in the same position as before the tort was committed. If damages were given for the time after he developed the disease he would be in a better position than if he had not been injured. The disease was one of the misfortunes of life. The defendant was only liable for damages up to 1976 when the claimant developed the disease.

The above two cases can be distinguished in as much as in *Baker* two successive torts are committed whereas in *Jobling* the second event is a disease.

## Loss of a chance

A claimant must prove their case on a balance of probability, that is, at least 51%. If they are unable to do this they will lose the case. In such a situation the question arises whether they can claim for the loss of chance. As regards the risks of treatment, a claimant only has to show that if they had been told the risks they would not have had the treatment 'at that time' *Chaudry Chester v Afshar* [2004] 1 AC 134.

### Case precedent – *Hotson v East Berks HA* [1987] 1 All ER 210

**Facts:** The claimant, a 13 year old boy, fell out of a tree. He was taken to hospital, examined and sent home. Five days later he went back to hospital and it was discovered that he had broken his hip. He developed a deformity of the hip. If he had been correctly diagnosed and treated when he first went to hospital he would have had a 25% chance of making a full recovery. The High Court awarded him 25% damages.

**Principle:** The House of Lords said that the claimant had to prove on a balance of probability that the delay caused the deformity. As he only had a 25% chance of recovery he could not do this and his claim failed.

**Application:** The approach taken by the House of Lords was strict that if the claimant could not prove his case on balance he got nothing. The same approach must be followed in applying the case in problem questions.

The House of Lords left open the question whether damages could ever be claimed for loss of a chance. In *Gregg v Scott* [2002] EWCA Civ 1471 the defendant doctor wrongly diagnosed a lump under the claimant's arm as harmless. A year later it was correctly diagnosed as malignant cancer. The claimant argued that if he had originally been diagnosed correctly when he first saw the doctor, he would have had a 42% chance of surviving for ten years. Now he only had a 25% chance. It was held by the House of Lords that he could not prove on a balance of probabilities that he would have survived ten years.

## Common Pitfall

If there is more than one cause of the harm the 'but for' test is not used. The test of material contribution can then be applied.

## New intervening acts

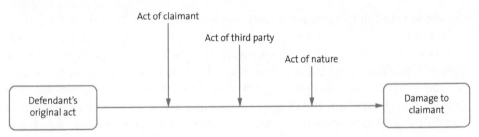

After the defendant's negligent act there may be a second act or event which also causes harm to the claimant. The second act may be sufficient to break the 'chain of causation' between the defendant's act and the harm to the claimant. If this is established, the second act is known as a new intervening act or *novus actus interveniens*. The effect is that the defendant is not liable for the later harm. The court has to decide whether the new act is serious enough to make it the cause of the damage rather than the defendant's original act. In *Hogan v Bentinck Collieries* [1949] 1 All ER 588 the claimant, a miner, fractured his thumb at work due to his employer's negligence. He went to hospital and the hospital amputated his thumb. It was held by the House of Lords that the amputation was not needed and it amounted to a new intervening act. The employer was not liable for the amputation but was liable for the original injury.

## Act of the claimant

If the claimant does an act after the defendant's negligent act which overrides the defendant's act, the result is that the claimant is liable for the harm. The test applied by the courts is – was the claimant's act unreasonable in all the circumstances?

### Case precedent – *McKew v Holland* [1969] 3 All ER 1621

**Facts:** Due to the negligence of the defendant the claimant suffered an injury to his left leg at work, which sometimes resulted in loss of control of the leg. Soon after the accident he was going down a steep flight of stairs which had no handrail, holding his grand-daughter's hand, when his left leg gave way. He tried to jump but fell and broke his ankle.

**Principle:** The House of Lords said that going down the stairs was unreasonable and amounted to a new intervening act. The defendant was not liable for the broken ankle.

**Application:** The test of what is reasonable applied to the claimant's acts is quite vague. The courts are trying to determine what would be fair in each case.

The above case can be contrasted with *Wieland v Cyril Lord Carpets* [1968] 3 All ER 1006. The claimant was injured due to the defendant's negligence and as a result had to wear a surgical collar, which meant she could not see properly with her glasses. A few days after the accident, she was going down a flight of stairs with her son when she fell and was injured. It was held that she could not manage without her glasses and the defendant was also liable for her later injuries. In *McKew* the claimant was acting unreasonably but in *Wieland* she was being reasonable.

One difficult issue arises if someone commits suicide following a negligent act by the defendant. Is the act of suicide a new intervening act? In *Corr v IBC Vehicles* [2008] UKHL 13 the claimant's husband suffered serious head injuries at work due to his employer's negligence. As a result he also suffered depression and six years later committed suicide. The House of Lords said that it was foreseeable the claimant would suffer depression as a result of the accident. Although committing suicide was the claimant's own act it was the result of the depression and was not a voluntary act. It was not a new intervening act and the defendant was liable in negligence.

## Act of a third party

After the defendant's negligent act a third party may commit a second negligent act which causes harm to the claimant. The question is whether this second act is enough to break the chain of causation. The courts take a number of factors into account such as whether the act is foreseeable; whether it is a voluntary act. There may even be a duty on the defendant to prevent a third party causing harm, for example, *Home Office v Dorset Yacht Co* [1970] AC 1004.

In *Scott v Shepherd* (1773) 2 Wm Bl 892 the defendant threw a firework into a market place and it landed near T's stall. T picked it up and threw it away. It landed near the claimant and exploded injuring him. Who should be liable, the defendant or T? The court said that T's act was foreseeable and was simply to protect himself. It was not a new intervening act and the defendant was liable for battery.

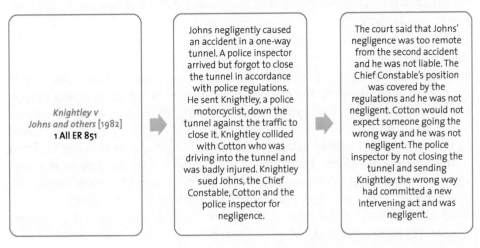

*Knightley v Johns and others* [1982] 1 All ER 851

Johns negligently caused an accident in a one-way tunnel. A police inspector arrived but forgot to close the tunnel in accordance with police regulations. He sent Knightley, a police motorcyclist, down the tunnel against the traffic to close it. Knightley collided with Cotton who was driving into the tunnel and was badly injured. Knightley sued Johns, the Chief Constable, Cotton and the police inspector for negligence.

The court said that Johns' negligence was too remote from the second accident and he was not liable. The Chief Constable's position was covered by the regulations and he was not negligent. Cotton would not expect someone going the wrong way and he was not negligent. The police inspector by not closing the tunnel and sending Knightley the wrong way had committed a new intervening act and was negligent.

In the above case the court accepted that mistakes can be made in a crisis. In deciding if the harm caused is too remote from the original accident decisions have to be made on the basis of common sense.

If the claimant is put in danger as a result of the defendant's negligence and someone tries to rescue the claimant but causes further harm will the rescuer's act be a new intervening act? In *The Oropesa* [1943] 1 All ER 211 the captain of *The Oropesa* negligently collided with another ship and damaged it. The captain of that ship set out in a lifeboat with some crew to consult the captain of *The Oropesa* about saving the damaged ship. The lifeboat capsized in heavy seas and some of the crew drowned. It was held by the Court of Appeal that given the dangerous position he was in, the captain's decision to set off in the lifeboat was not a new intervening act. The captain of *The Oropesa* remained liable in negligence for the deaths.

If as a result of the defendant's negligence the claimant needs medical treatment and that treatment is negligent, will it break the chain of causation? It is foreseeable that if the claimant is injured the claimant will need medical treatment and it is also foreseeable that such treatment could be given negligently. The medical treatment would have to be grossly negligent to break the chain of causation. In *Wright v Cambridge Medical Group* [2011] EWCA Civ 669 a child contracted an infection and the child's mother telephoned her GP to report the symptoms but the GP did not take any action. Two days later a GP visited the child and referred her to hospital immediately. At the hospital the child was not correctly diagnosed and treated until five days after being admitted. As a result she sustained permanent damage to her hip from the infection. She sued the GP for negligence which the GP admitted but denied liability for the permanent damage to her hip. The Court of Appeal said that there was a presumption that if she had been referred to hospital immediately she would have received competent treatment. The delay had reduced the time for the hospital to treat her successfully and the GP had failed to change that presumption and was liable for all the damage including the permanent damage.

## Act of nature

After the defendant's negligent act further harm may be caused to the claimant or their property by an act of nature, for example, a storm or lightning. Does a natural event break the chain of causation? In *Carslogie Steamship Co v Royal Norwegian Government* [1952] AC 292 the claimant's ship was damaged in a collision caused by the defendant. The ship sailed to the United States for repairs but suffered further damage in a storm. The claimant argued that but for the defendant's negligence the ship would not have had to sail to the United States and would not have suffered storm damage. The House of Lords held that the storm broke the chain of causation and the defendant was not liable for the further damage and loss of income from charters.

# Legal causation

Even when it has been established that the defendant's negligent act has factually caused the harm to the claimant it still has to be determined as a matter of law, whether the defendant should be liable. The test to decide this is the test of remoteness; if the damage is too remote from the defendant's act the defendant will not be liable. The reason for this test is to draw a line where the defendant's liability stops.

## Test of reasonable foreseeability

The original test for deciding if the damage was too remote was the 'direct consequences' test. This makes the defendant liable for all consequences which can be directly linked to the defendant's negligent act, whether they are foreseeable or not (*Re Polemis* [1921] 3 KB 560). This test was replaced by the test of 'reasonable foreseeability' in the following case.

## Case precedent – *The Wagon Mound (No 1)* [1961] AC 388

**Facts:** The defendants carelessly spilled oil from their tanker into Sydney Harbour. The claimants were welding at their dock about 200 metres away and stopped when oil was seen along the dock. The claimants were told that it was safe to continue welding as it was believed that the oil would not burn on water. Molten metal from the welding fell on to some cotton rag soaked with oil in the water and a fire started which damaged the dock.

**Principle:** The Privy Council said that it was not reasonably foreseeable that the dock would catch fire as a result of the defendant's negligent act. The defendant was not liable.

**Application:** This case established the principle that damage must be reasonably foreseeable. But this has been qualified by *Hughes v Lord Advocate* [1963] AC 837.

## Kind of damage

The defendant will only be liable if the type or kind of damage suffered was reasonably foreseeable. In *The Wagon Mound (No 1)* [1961] although physical damage from the oil fouling the dock was foreseeable, damage by fire was not foreseeable and was therefore too remote. The defendant does not have to foresee the extent of the damage.

How the wording for the test of the kind of damage is phrased, will have an effect on the outcome of the test. In *Hughes v Lord Advocate* [1963] AC 837 some Post Office employees were working down a manhole in the street. They put a tent over the manhole, four paraffin lamps around it and went off for a cup of tea. Two boys aged eight and ten went up to the manhole and started playing with a paraffin lamp. The claimant knocked the lamp into the manhole, the paraffin turned into a vapour, was ignited by the flame and caused an explosion. The claimant was badly burned. The defendant argued that this chain of events was very unusual and an explosion could not be foreseen, so they were not liable. The House of Lords said that it was foreseeable that children might play with the lamps and that paraffin might spill and cause a fire. Whether the burning is caused by liquid paraffin or paraffin which has vaporised, they both cause burns. The claimant had suffered a foreseeable type of harm, burning. The defendant was liable in negligence. The House of Lords said that the accident was caused by a known source of danger, the lamp. Lord Jenkins said,

'the distinction drawn between burning and explosion is too fine to warrant acceptance'.

A contrasting approach was taken in *Doughty v Turner Manufacturing* [1964] 1 QB 518. The defendant had a bath of sodium cyanide heated to 800 degrees centigrade. The bath had a lid made of asbestos. The lid was carelessly knocked into the bath and it reacted with the sodium cyanide and caused an explosion. The claimant, who was standing nearby, was burned. The Court of Appeal said that the type of injury foreseeable if the lid was knocked into the bath was injury by splashing with the chemical. Here the chemical reaction was not foreseeable because at the time no one knew asbestos would react with the chemical and the defendant was not liable.

*Doughty* takes a narrow view of what was foreseeable. If the type of harm was injury by 'burning' the defendant would have been liable. The courts now seem to be taking a wider view of the foreseeable harm. In *Jolley v Sutton LBC* [2000] 3 All ER 409 the House of Lords identified the harm as some physical injury from meddling with the boat (see Chapter 7).

## Aim Higher

Read *Hughes v Lord Advocate* [1963] and in particular the judgment of Lord Guest and his statement about paraffin vapour and liquid paraffin.

The result is that if the kind of damage is foreseeable the claimant can recover. It is not necessary for the defendant to foresee the exact chain of events or the extent of the damage.

Does liability therefore depend on how the damage is defined?

## Common Pitfall

Remember that in proving causation there are two steps. It is an easy mistake to deal with factual causation but ignore legal causation and the test of remoteness.

## The eggshell skull rule

If the type of harm is foreseeable the eggshell skull rule says that if the claimant, due to some sensitivity, suffers greater harm than a normal person, the defendant is liable for that harm. The principle behind this rule is that you take your victim as you find them.

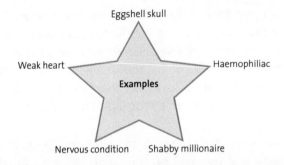

**Case precedent – *Smith v Leech Brain* [1962] 2 QB 405**

**Facts:** The claimant's husband worked in the defendant's ironworks. In 1950 due to the carelessness of his employers a drop of molten metal splashed on to his lip causing a small burn. This was treated. Sometime after this the burn caused a dormant cancer to develop and he died in 1953. The defendants argued that it was not reasonably foreseeable that the husband would die of cancer as a result of a small burn.

**Principle:** The court said that the defendant could foresee the type of harm, a burn, and was therefore fully liable for his death.

**Application:** This rule protects the vulnerable claimant. In problem questions it is important to check whether any claimant has a vulnerability.

The eggshell skull rule was applied in the following case. In *Robinson v Post Office* [1974] 2 All ER 737 due to the defendant's negligence the claimant slipped on an oily ladder at work and cut his leg. He went to hospital and was given an anti-tetanus injection by a doctor but had an allergic reaction to the vaccine and suffered brain damage. The doctor was at fault for not waiting for the result of an allergy test but the test would not have revealed the allergy. The defendants argued that they were only liable for the injury to the leg. The Court of Appeal said that it was reasonably foreseeable that if the claimant was cut he would need medical treatment. The defendant was liable for the original injury and the consequences of that medical treatment even though these were not foreseeable.

## Putting it into practice

Please read both Chapter 2 and Chapter 3 before attempting the following question.

Gina, a city banker, owns a small single engine plane. She was not paid a bonus one year and as she was short of money she failed to have her plane serviced. One afternoon she was flying back to the airport in her plane when the engine failed because it had not been serviced. Gina was forced to land on a road and she collided with a car being driven by Haroon. Haroon was badly cut in the accident and Gina called the ambulance service on her mobile phone. Haroon was taken to hospital and Ivy, a newly qualified nurse, seeing that Haroon had been cut gave him an anti-tetanus injection. This caused him to suffer brain damage.

Jack lives in a house overlooking the road and he heard the crash. He went to see what was happening and was first on the scene. He went to help Haroon but slipped in some leaking aviation fuel from the plane and broke his leg.

Ken owns a garage 300 metres downhill from the scene of the crash. He was welding when leaking aviation fuel, which had flowed down the hill from the scene of the crash, was ignited by the flame from the welding and started a fire. The fire burned down the garage.

**Advise Haroon, Jack and Ken of any claims they may make in negligence.**

## Outline answer – negligence, duty, breach and causation

❖ *Haroon v Gina*

    ❖ Negligence: does Gina owe a duty of care to Haroon? *Caparo* test: foreseeability. Is it foreseeable that if Gina does not service her plane it will go wrong? Proximity: both on the road. Fair, just and reasonableness, Gina has insurance.

    ❖ Breach of duty: Gina not servicing the plane is an omission (not doing something) but it is part of a course of conduct which is flying the plane. *Bolam* test: would a competent pilot fail to service the plane?

    ❖ Causation: did the breach cause the harm? Haroon's cuts: 'but for' test, *Barnett v Chelsea & Kensington HMC*; he would not have suffered the cuts but for Gina's negligence, but consider the effect of Ivy's act.

❖ *Haroon v Ivy*

    ❖ Ivy owes a duty of care to patients; is she in breach? *Bolam* test: a competent nurse; the fact she is newly qualified does not matter; would a competent nurse have tested Haroon for allergies first?

    ❖ Is it a new intervening act which overrides the original negligence of Gina? *Knightley v Johns*. It is foreseeable that an injured claimant will need medical treatment but the treatment would have to be grossly negligent to break the chain of causation.

❖ It would seem that Gina remains liable; under the eggshell skull rule, *Smith v Leech Brain* she is liable for the brain damage as well as the cuts.

❖ *Jack v Gina*

  ❖ Negligence: does Gina owe a duty of care to Jack? Is it foreseeable that if Gina is negligent and causes an accident someone would come to help? There is proximity as Jack is at the scene. It is also just and reasonable that a duty is owed as Gina will have insurance. Is Gina in breach of her duty? *Bolam* test; also causation; test of remoteness; has Gina's breach caused harm to Jack? *Chadwick v British Railways Board* [1967] 1 WLR 912, Gina is liable.

❖ *Ken v Gina*

  ❖ Negligence: does Gina owe a duty of care to Ken? *Caparo* test: this could be arguable as not being foreseeable or proximate; but the facts of highly flammable aviation fuel and the garage down a hill it could be argued the other way.
  ❖ Breach: Gina is in breach of her duty by not servicing the plane.
  ❖ Causation. Factual causation: but for Gina's negligence the fire would not have happened. Legal causation: is the garage catching fire too remote from the plane crash? The kind of harm is foreseeable, damage by fire; Ken's situation may be distinguished from the *Wagon Mound (No 1)* where it was not foreseeable that the oil would burn. It is likely that Gina would be found negligent.

# Table of key cases referred to in this chapter

| Key case | Area of law | Principle |
|---|---|---|
| *Barnett v Chelsea & Kensington HMC* [1969] 1 QB 428 | A night watchman died of arsenic poisoning after being turned away from hospital. Hospital not liable. | 'But for' test to show factual causation; the night watchman would have died even if admitted to hospital. |
| *Hotson v East Berks HA* [1987] 1 All ER 210 | Boy with broken hip not diagnosed correctly. Only 25% chance of full recovery; hospital not negligent. | Claimant must prove case on a balance of probabilities, at least 51%. |
| *Hughes v Lord Advocate* [1963] AC 837 | Paraffin in lamp exploded and burned boy. Defendants argued they could not foresee explosion; but liable in negligence as could foresee burning. | Claimant must prove that the type of harm suffered was foreseeable. |

| Key case | Area of law | Principle |
|---|---|---|
| *Knightley v Johns* [1982] 1 All ER 851 | A police inspector (third party) forgot to close tunnel after a road accident. He sent a police motorcyclist the wrong way down the tunnel and caused another accident. | Act of third party after original negligent act may break the chain of causation. |
| *McGhee v NCB* [1972] 3 All ER 1008 | The claimant got a skin disease from brick dust but was unable to prove it was from the dust on the way home rather than the dust during the day. | The defendant had 'materially increased' the risk of disease and was negligent. This test is used if 'but for' test does not work. |
| *McKew v Holland* [1969] 3 All ER 1621 | Defendant negligently injured claimant's leg but later claimant went down steep stairs, fell when leg gave way and broke his ankle. | Claimant's act of going down stairs was unreasonable and a new intervening act. Defendant not liable for broken ankle. |
| *Smith v Leech Brain* [1962] 2 QB 405 | Defendant negligently caused burn on lip which led to cancer developing and claimant's husband died. | The eggshell skull rule applied. The defendant was liable for the claimant's death even though this was unforeseeable. |
| *The Wagon Mound (No 1)* [1961] AC 388 (*Overseas Tankship Ltd v Morts Docks Co*) | The defendants negligently spilled oil into the harbour; it was set on fire by the claimant's welding and burned down their dock. Defendants were not liable. | The test of reasonable foreseeability was applied to establish legal causation. It was not reasonably foreseeable that the oil would burn and the dock would go on fire. |

@  **Visit the book's companion website to test your knowledge**

❖  Resources include a subject map, revision tip podcasts, downloadable diagrams, MCQ quizzes for each chapter and a flashcard glossary

❖  www.routledge.com/cw/optimizelawrevision

# 4

# Negligence: Economic Loss, Negligent Mis-statement and Psychiatric Injury

## Revision objectives

**Understand the law**
- Can you define what is meant by pure economic loss and consequential economic loss?
- Can you explain the importance of *Murphy v Brentwood District Council*?
- Can you define a negligent mis-statement?
- Can you define what a psychiatric injury is and give three examples?
- Can you distinguish a primary victim from a secondary victim?

**Remember the details**
- Can you identify and explain the three claims in *Spartan Steel v Martin*?
- Can you define the three requirements to establish a negligent mis-statement?
- Can you explain what must be established for a third party to rely on a negligent mis-statement?
- Can you explain the wills cases and why these are an exception to the general rule on economic loss?
- Can you explain the tree requirements from *Alcock* which a secondary victim must establish?

**Reflect critically on areas of debate**
- Can you assess the difficulties of applying the three criteria from *Hedley Byrne v Heller*?
- Can you discuss the arguments for and against changing the law on secondary victims of psychiatric injury?

**Contextualise**
- Do you understand the policy reasons why claims for economic loss and negligent mis-statements are restricted?
- Do you understand how restrictive the *Alcock* rules are for secondary victims of psychiatric injury?

**Apply your skills and knowledge**
- Can you answer the question at the end of this chapter?

# Chapter Map

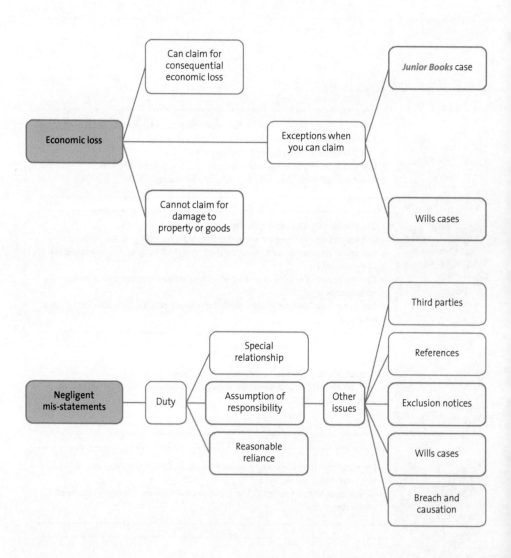

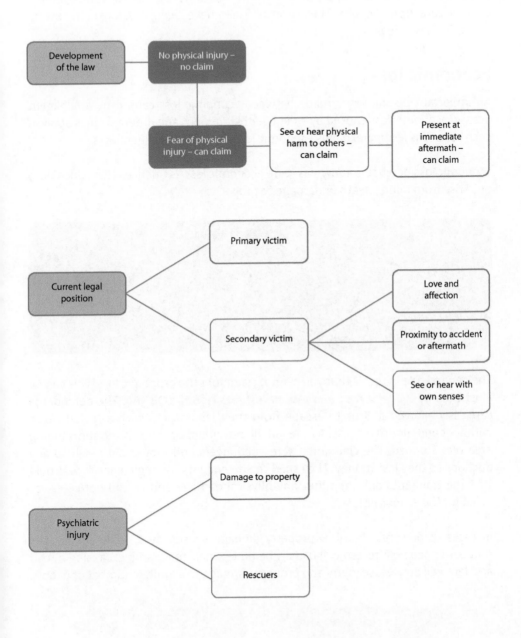

# Introduction

The law of negligence has developed special rules for the three areas covered in this chapter. These rules apply in addition to the universal test for establishing a duty of care from *Caparo*. These special rules have been developed to restrict claims in these areas.

# Economic loss

An important distinction is made between economic loss caused by a negligent act and economic loss caused by a negligent statement and different rules apply in each case. This section explains economic loss caused by negligent acts.

Economic loss or what is known as 'pure economic loss' is financial loss which does not arise from injury, death or damage to property.

## Example

Ann drives negligently and causes an accident on the motorway which results in a traffic jam.

Ben's car is caught in the traffic jam and he is late for work and loses two hours' pay. Ben's loss is pure economic loss.

The general rule in tort is that you cannot claim for pure economic loss. This can be illustrated by *Weller v Foot and Mouth Institute* [1966] 1 QB 569. The defendants carelessly allowed a virus to escape from their laboratory which affected cattle with foot and mouth disease. As a result all movement of cattle in the surrounding area was stopped. The claimants were auctioneers and they could not hold any auctions so they lost money. They sued the defendants for negligence. It was held that the claimants did not suffer any physical damage and no duty of care was owed for the economic loss.

In cases of personal injury or property damage caused by a negligent act the number of people affected will usually be quite small, for example, causing a road accident will only cause injury and property damage to a limited number of people.

Pure economic loss cannot claim

Consequential economic loss can claim

In contrast economic loss may affect a large number of people. For example if the electricity supply to a town is cut off thousands of people will suffer economic loss.

The courts, as a matter of policy, have therefore restricted such claims because of worries that there would be a flood of claims.

| Pure economic loss | Consequential economic loss |
|---|---|
| The only loss you suffer is financial<br><br>Cannot claim | As a result of a negligent act you suffer injury or physical damage to property and as a result (or consequence) of this also suffer economic loss<br><br>Can claim for this consequential economic loss |

### Case precedent – *Spartan Steel v Martin Ltd* [1973] 1 QB 27

**Facts:** The defendants negligently cut the electricity cable to the claimant's steel foundry. The claimants claimed for: (i) damage to metal in the furnace which solidified and had to be thrown away; (ii) loss of profit on that metal; (iii) loss of profit on 'melts' which could have been processed while the foundry was closed.

**Principle:** The Court of Appeal held that the claimants could claim for (i), which was physical damage, and for (ii), which was consequential economic loss following from the physical damage to the metal in the furnace. They could not claim for (iii), which was pure economic loss, caused by the electricity supply being cut off.

**Application:** This case provides a clear example of how the rules on economic loss apply. If Spartan Steel had owned the electricity cable they could have also claimed for the loss of profit while the factory was closed.

There was physical damage to the electricity cable but the cable was owned by the electricity board. To claim for consequential economic loss the damage must be to the defendant or to their property.

## Defective property

If someone buys goods or property which has a defect the cost of fixing it is pure economic loss. The traditional view was that you could not claim for that in tort. However, the courts took a different view in *Anns v Merton London Borough Council* [1978] AC 728. The claimant bought a flat. Some years later cracks appeared in the walls and it was found that this was caused by defective foundations. The claimant sued the local authority for negligence for carelessly inspecting the foundations. It was held by the House of Lords that the cracks were physical damage to the building so it was not just pure economic loss. There was imminent danger to the health of the occupiers and the defendant was liable in negligence.

This decision was applied in *Junior Books v Veitchi* [1983] 1 AC 520. The claimants entered a contract with the main contractor to build a factory and told them to employ the defendants who were specialists, to lay the floor. The floor was laid negligently and the factory had to close while it was relaid. The claimant did not have a contract with the defendants and sued in negligence for the cost of relaying the floor and for the loss of profit while the factory was closed. The House of Lords said that the defendants knew the claimants relied on their skill and it was foreseeable that the claimant would suffer loss if the defendants acted negligently. The relationship between the claimant and defendant was 'almost a contract' and there was close proximity. The defendants were liable.

These two cases showed that at that time the tort of negligence was expanding and covering new claims which previously could only be made in contract. The courts later began to restrict the law of negligence. In *Murphy v Brentwood District Council* [1990] 1 AC 398 the House of Lords overruled *Anns* and restricted claims for economic loss.

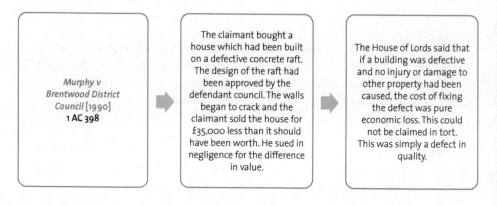

*Murphy v Brentwood District Council* [1990] 1 AC 398

The claimant bought a house which had been built on a defective concrete raft. The design of the raft had been approved by the defendant council. The walls began to crack and the claimant sold the house for £35,000 less than it should have been worth. He sued in negligence for the difference in value.

The House of Lords said that if a building was defective and no injury or damage to other property had been caused, the cost of fixing the defect was pure economic loss. This could not be claimed in tort. This was simply a defect in quality.

The above cases relate to defective property but the same rules apply to defective goods. In *Muirhead v Industrial Tank Specialities* [1985] 3 All ER 705 the claimant, a fish merchant, had a plan to buy lobsters cheap in the summer, keep them in tanks and sell them when the price went up in the winter. The claimant bought electric pumps for the tanks from a supplier but the pumps did not work properly because they were the wrong voltage for the UK. The supplier went bankrupt. The claimant sued the manufacturer for negligence. He claimed:

❖ the cost of the lobsters that died in the tanks and loss of profit on them;
❖ money spent trying to fix the pumps; and
❖ loss of profit on the business as a whole.

The Court of Appeal said that he could claim for

❖ the lobsters which was damage to other property and loss of profit on them which was consequential economic loss; but not for:

- ❖ money fixing pumps; and
- ❖ loss of profit on the business, which were both pure economic loss.

The claimant could not prove that he had relied on the manufacturer.

The result is that claims for loss arising from defective property can only be made in contract.

## Common Pitfall

It is sometimes easy to miss economic loss problem questions and answer them on the basis of the normal rules of negligence. If you identify a loss which does not have any physical injury or damage to property that is the pointer to economic loss.

## Exceptions to the rule no claim can be made for economic loss

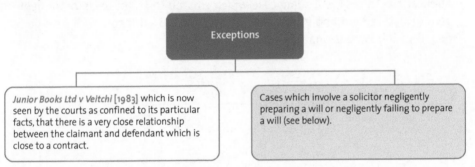

*Junior Books Ltd v Veitchi* [1983] which is now seen by the courts as confined to its particular facts, that there is a very close relationship between the claimant and defendant which is close to a contract.

Cases which involve a solicitor negligently preparing a will or negligently failing to prepare a will (see below).

# Negligent mis-statements

A negligent mis-statement can have more far reaching effects than a negligent act and the courts have developed special rules to deal with such statements. For example, a negligent mis-statement made on a television programme advising people to invest in a specific company could be acted on by thousands of people who all lose money as a result.

The original rule in tort was that no claim could be made for a negligent statement. A claim could only be made for a fraudulent statement, which is a statement made knowing it is false or recklessly, without caring whether it is true or false, *Derry v Peek* (1889) 14 App Cas 337.

This rule was changed in *Hedley Byrne v Heller* [1964] which established a duty in respect of a negligent mis-statement. The claimant also has to prove breach of duty and that the breach caused the loss.

## Case precedent – *Hedley Byrne v Heller* [1964] AC 465

**Facts:** The claimant advertising agents wished to enter a contract with E Ltd. The claimants asked NPBank, their own bank, to find out about E Ltd. NPBank contacted the defendant, E Ltd's bank, who sent a letter stating that E Ltd were good for 'ordinary business engagements'. The letter also stated that the advice was given 'without responsibility'. The letter was shown to the claimant who entered a contract with E Ltd. E Ltd later went into liquidation and the claimant lost £17,000. At the time the defendant gave the reference E Ltd were heavily overdrawn. The claimant sued for negligent mis-statement.

**Principle:** On the facts it was held by the House of Lords that the defendant owed a duty of care to the claimant but was not liable because of the exemption clause in the letter. The House set out the principles for liability in such circumstances.

**Application:** This is the leading case which created the right to claim for negligent mis-statement and it has been used to impose a duty on a wide range of people giving professional advice.

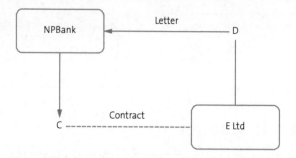

## Requirements for a duty for negligent mis-statement

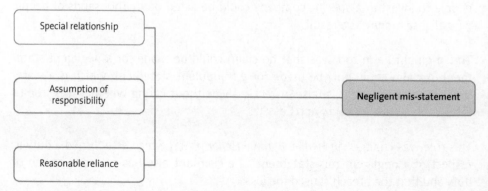

## Special relationship

A special relationship will arise if the person giving the information knows that the other party is relying on the information. It will normally arise in business situations. The person who gives the advice does not have to give advice as part of their job like an accountant or a solicitor. It is sufficient to give the advice in the course of a business.

In *Patchett v Swimming Pool Association* [2009] EWCA Civ 717 the defendants were a trade association and had a website with a list of swimming pool installers. The website advised people to obtain an information pack from the defendants and to make their own independent enquiries. The claimant chose an installer from the list and entered a contract with them. The installer became insolvent before completing the swimming pool and the claimants lost money. The installer was not a full member of the association. The claimant sued the defendant for negligent mis-statement. The Court of Appeal said that there was not sufficient proximity between the claimant and defendant to create a special relationship. Neither had the SPA assumed responsibility to the claimant because the claimant had not obtained an information pack which would have told them the installer was not a full member and they had not made their own enquiries. It was held by a 2/1 majority that the defendant did not owe a duty to the claimant.

In contrast to advice given in the course of a business, advice given on a social occasion will not generally lead to liability, for example, giving someone advice at a party about what shares to buy. This rule must be seen in the light of the following decision.

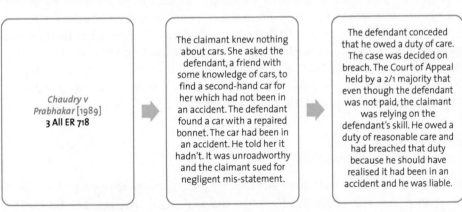

*Chaudry v Prabhakar* [1989] 3 All ER 718 → The claimant knew nothing about cars. She asked the defendant, a friend with some knowledge of cars, to find a second-hand car for her which had not been in an accident. The defendant found a car with a repaired bonnet. The car had been in an accident. He told her it hadn't. It was unroadworthy and the claimant sued for negligent mis-statement. → The defendant conceded that he owed a duty of care. The case was decided on breach. The Court of Appeal held by a 2/1 majority that even though the defendant was not paid, the claimant was relying on the defendant's skill. He owed a duty of reasonable care and had breached that duty because he should have realised it had been in an accident and he was liable.

A dissenting judgment was given by May LJ who argued that it was not right to impose such a duty on a friend and doing so would make social arrangements 'unnecessarily hazardous'.

## Aim Higher

Read the above case *Chaudry v Prabhakar* and the dissenting judgment of May LJ. The case explains the social circumstances when someone could be liable for a negligent mis-statement and will enable you to apply your knowledge in problem questions.

## Voluntary assumption of responsibility

To establish an assumption of responsibility it is not enough that the defendant can foresee that the claimant will be given the information. Assumption of responsibility is about showing proximity between the defendant and the claimant. An auditor of accounts can foresee that the public may see those accounts but does the auditor owe a duty to the public. In *Caparo v Dickman* [1990] 1 All ER 568 the claimant owned shares in F Ltd. The claimant saw the accounts of F Ltd which had been audited by the defendants and given to F Ltd's AGM and then bought a majority of the shares. It was later found that although the accounts showed a profit of £1.3 million F Ltd had made a loss of £465,000. The claimant sued for negligent mis-statement. It was held by the House of Lords that the purpose of the audit was to protect the shareholders of F Ltd as a group from mismanagement. If the audit was carried out negligently a claim could be made by the shareholders in the name of the company. No duty was owed to the claimant as an individual existing shareholder or as a member of the public.

In *Merrett v Babb* [2001] EWCA Civ 214 the claimant wished to buy a house. Her building society asked a firm of surveyors to conduct a valuation. The defendant surveyor, an employee of the firm, carelessly valued the house for the building society and the valuation was given to the claimant who then bought the house. The claimant later discovered that the house had lots of defects but the firm had gone into liquidation. She sued the surveyor personally. It was held by the Court of Appeal by a 2/1 majority that the defendant should have realised that the claimant buyer would rely on his skill. He had signed the valuation report and therefore assumed responsibility for it. He was liable even though he had no insurance!

## Reasonable reliance

The claimant must show that:

❖  they relied on the statement and that it was reasonable to rely on it;
❖  they relied on the defendant's skill or knowledge and they acted on the basis of the advice; and
❖  they must also show that it was reasonable to rely on the defendant.

In *Caparo v Dickman* [1990] the claimant relied on the audited accounts prepared by the defendants for a company AGM and on the basis of the accounts bought shares in the company. The accounts were inaccurate and the claimant lost money. However, it was not reasonable to rely on the accounts which had been produced for the benefit of the shareholders as a group.

## Negligent mis-statements and third parties

If a statement is made by the defendant to one person but a third party relies on it, can the third party claim under *Hedley Byrne v Heller*?

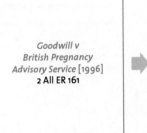

| *Goodwill v British Pregnancy Advisory Service* [1996] 2 All ER 161 | ➡ | M, a married man, had a vasectomy carried out by the defendant, who told him he did not need to use contraception. Three years later he began a relationship with the claimant and told her about his vasectomy. However, the vasectomy reversed naturally and the claimant became pregnant by M and had a baby. She sued the defendant for the negligent statement to M and claimed the cost of bringing up the baby. | ➡ | The Court of Appeal said that, first, when the advice was given to M the claimant was one of a large class of future sexual partners and she could not show that the defendants had assumed responsibility to her. Second, she could not show the defendant knew the advice would be acted on without independent enquiry. Third, she had to show she had acted to her detriment. The defendant was not liable. |

The doctor carrying out a sterilisation would owe a duty of care to the patient's existing partner but not to future partners. Since this case a man or woman who is sterilised will be told that the operation is not 100% effective and can be reversed naturally by the body. This warning would prevent claims for negligent mis-statement.

## Negligent mis-statements and references

An employer providing a reference for an ex-employee owes a duty of care to that employee to do it without negligence. In *Spring v Guardian Assurance plc* [1995] 2 AC 296 the claimant was employed by the defendant but was dismissed. The defendant provided a reference to a potential new employer which stated that the claimant was dishonest and he failed to get the job. It was held by the House of Lords that the claimant was incompetent rather than dishonest and the defendant had been negligent in writing the reference. In *Hedley Byrne* the negligent mis-statement was given to someone who relied on it and suffered economic loss but in *Spring* although the mis-statement was not given to the claimant it caused him economic loss.

## Exclusion clauses

When the defendant makes the negligent mis-statement they may seek to rely on an exclusion clause or disclaimer as in *Hedley Byrne v Heller* [1964]. Whether this is successful will depend on whether it is used between businesses or a trader and a consumer. The Consumer Rights Act 2015 provides in s62 that any contract term or notice which is unfair is not binding on the consumer.

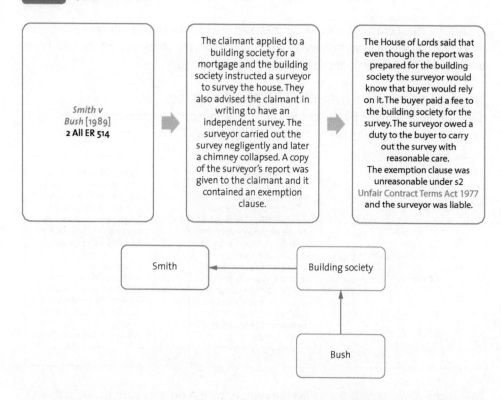

In *Smith v Bush* [1989] the court said that the buyer was purchasing a modest house and could not afford an independent survey. Someone buying a very expensive house or a commercial property would be expected to have their own survey. In *Scullion v Bank of Scotland (t/a Colleys)* [2011] EWCA Civ 693 the claimant bought a buy-to-let flat after seeing the valuation prepared for the lender. The valuation was negligent and the flat was sold for £80,000 less than stated. The Court of Appeal held that it was a commercial transaction and buyers would be expected to have their own survey. The defendants owed no duty to the claimant.

## The wills cases

Cases involving wills do not fit in with the principles under *Hedley Byrne v Heller* [1964] as it is difficult to show that the claimant beneficiaries put reliance on the solicitors or that the solicitors assumed responsibility towards the claimants. The claimants may not even know that they had been left gifts in the will. Also the claims are not based on negligent statements but on a service performed negligently.

In *Ross v Caunters* [1980] Ch 297 the claimant's husband witnessed a will in which the claimant was a beneficiary. The defendant solicitor did not tell the testator that the gift would fail because under the Wills Act 1837 s15 a beneficiary whose spouse witnesses the will loses their gift. The claimant sued the solicitor for the economic loss caused by negligence. The House of Lords said that as the claimant was a named beneficiary, it was foreseeable that she would suffer loss and there was also proximity. Imposing liability would not lead to unlimited liability as only beneficiaries could claim. The solicitor was liable.

In *White v Jones* [1995] 1 All ER 691 the 78 year old testator quarrelled with the claimants, his daughters, and told the defendant solicitors to make a will leaving them out. The testator then made friends with his daughters and told the solicitors to make a new will including his daughters. The solicitors delayed and missed meetings with the testator, who then died. The claimants sued for negligence. The House of Lords by a majority of 3/2 held that the defendants were liable in negligence as otherwise the claimants would have no remedy.

# Psychiatric injury

## Introduction
A psychiatric injury is an injury which affects the claimant's mind as opposed to a physical injury which is an injury to their body. In the past the courts have used the term 'nervous shock' but it is now common to use psychiatric injury. If a claimant wishes to sue in negligence for psychiatric injury they must prove that they have suffered a recognised psychiatric illness.

A distinction is made between a recognised psychiatric injury and mere distress or normal grief and sorrow which everyone is expected to accept as part of life and for which no claims can be made.

The claimant must also show that a person of 'normal fortitude' (or ordinary phlegm) would have suffered psychiatric injury in the circumstances. This means someone with normal courage who faces a traumatic event.

## Development of the law
The original rule in negligence was that you could not claim for psychiatric injury. A claim could be made for psychiatric injury if there was also a physical injury. In *Victorian Railway Commissioners v Coultas* (1888) 13 App Cas 222 the claimant suffered nervous shock but the Privy Council held that without also suffering a physical injury her claim failed.

The courts made a step forwards in the next case when they allowed a claim for psychiatric injury even though there was no physical harm caused.

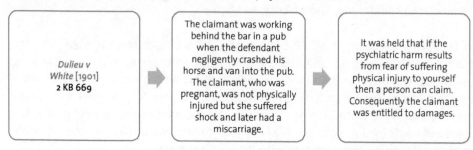

| *Dulieu v White* [1901] 2 KB 669 | → | The claimant was working behind the bar in a pub when the defendant negligently crashed his horse and van into the pub. The claimant, who was pregnant, was not physically injured but she suffered shock and later had a miscarriage. | → | It was held that if the psychiatric harm results from fear of suffering physical injury to yourself then a person can claim. Consequently the claimant was entitled to damages. |

The next step was to allow a claim when there was no danger of physical harm to the claimant. In *Hambrook v Stokes* [1925] 1 KB 141 the defendant left his lorry unattended with the handbrake off and it ran down a steep hill round a corner. The claimant had just left her children round the corner. She heard the crash and suffered nervous shock when she was told about an injured child who fitted the description of her daughter. The Court of Appeal held by a 2/1 majority that there could only be liability if the claimant saw or heard the event with their own senses. The mother was entitled to damages.

In *McLoughlin v O'Brien* [1983] AC 410 the claimant's family were involved in a road accident. One child was killed and the rest of the family were badly injured. At the time of the accident the claimant was at home two miles away. She was told about it by a friend and arrived at the hospital within two hours of the accident to see her family covered in oil and blood. She suffered clinical depression and sued the defendant who caused the accident. It was held by the House of Lords that although the claimant had not seen or heard the accident she had seen the 'immediate aftermath' and was entitled to damages. Lord Wilberforce set out the requirements for a claim: the class of persons who could claim; the need for proximity to the accident or the aftermath; and the means by which the claimant knew of the event.

## Distinction between primary and secondary victims
The law makes an important distinction between primary and secondary victims of psychiatric injury.

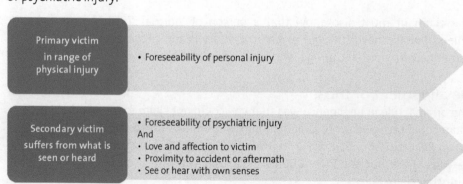

| Primary victim in range of physical injury | • Foreseeability of personal injury |
| Secondary victim suffers from what is seen or heard | • Foreseeability of psychiatric injury And<br>• Love and affection to victim<br>• Proximity to accident or aftermath<br>• See or hear with own senses |

## Primary victim

A primary victim is someone who is directly involved in the accident and within range of foreseeable personal injury.

The distinction between primary and secondary victims was first set out in *Page v Smith* [1996] 3 All ER 272. The defendant negligently crashed into the claimant's car at a low speed and neither driver suffered any physical injury. However, the accident caused the claimant's ME to return, which made him very tired and unable to work. ME is classed as a psychiatric injury. The House of Lords said that the claimant was a primary victim and only had to prove that the defendant could foresee 'personal injury' not injury by shock which was the requirement at that time. Personal injury was foreseeable even in a minor road accident and the defendant was liable.

The requirement of foreseeing personal injury makes it easier to claim because it is wider than just psychiatric injury and also covers physical injury.

The result is that a victim within range of physical injury who only suffers psychiatric injury can claim.

## Secondary victim

A secondary victim is someone who is not directly involved in an accident but suffers as a result of what they see or hear. Secondary victims are a much wider category than primary victims, who are limited to those at risk of physical harm. As a result the law has developed special rules to restrict who may claim. The test of foreseeability with secondary victims is foreseeability of psychiatric injury, that is, injury by shock. These rules were set out in *Alcock* [1992].

> ### Case precedent – *Alcock v Chief Constable of South Yorkshire* [1992] 4 All ER 907
>
> **Facts:** The defendants let too many fans into a football match at the Hillsborough Stadium in Sheffield resulting in the death of 96 people. The claimants, who included a range of relations and friends, suffered psychiatric harm and sued for negligence. Some were in the football ground, some saw the events live on the television or heard it on the radio and some identified dead bodies at the mortuary. They were all secondary victims.
>
> **Principle:** The House of Lords said that all the claims failed because they did not meet the criteria laid down by the court. Claimants had to have a relationship of love and affection to the victim, proximity to the accident or aftermath, and see or hear it with their own senses.
>
> **Application:** This case set out the criteria for secondary victims to claim which are still followed. The courts are still defining the scope of the criteria.

## Common Pitfall

It is important to remember the different tests of foreseeability for primary and secondary victims.

Primary victims – the test is foreseeability of 'personal injury'.

Secondary victims – the test is foreseeability of psychiatric injury which is a much narrower test.

## What secondary victims must establish

Love and affection between claimant and victim

Proximity of claimant to accident or aftermath

Must see or hear accident with own senses

### Relationship between the claimant and the victim

The court did not define the categories of relationship, for example, parent and child. The important factor was a relationship of 'love and affection' between the claimant and the victim. It had to be foreseeable that the victim would suffer psychiatric harm.

There was a presumption that such a relationship existed between spouses and between parents and children. This would also apply to engaged couples, civil partnerships and same sex marriages. However, this presumption could be rebutted by evidence to the contrary. In other relationships love and affection had to be proved, for example, if a child was brought up by their grandmother. In *Alcock* Lord Ackner said 'The quality of brotherly love is well known to differ widely.'

The claimants in *Alcock* included a brother and other relatives but all the claims failed as they were unable to establish a close tie of love and affection. The House of Lords left open the possibility of a claim by a bystander if they witnessed an horrific event and discussed the example of a petrol tanker crashing into a school and bursting into flames.

### Proximity of claimant to the accident or aftermath

This requirement is that the claimant must actually see the accident or the immediate aftermath. In *Alcock* some of the claimants were in the ground, some saw the events on television and some identified bodies of their relatives in mortuaries eight hours after the event, but none of them were able to claim. In *McLoughlin v O'Brien* [1983] the claimant went to the hospital two hours after the accident and was successful in her claim for psychiatric injury.

The exact scope of this requirement is flexible. In *W v Essex County Council* [2000] 2 All ER 237 the claimants wished to foster a child and told the defendants that they did not want someone with a history of committing child abuse. The defendants placed a 15 year old boy, whom they knew had committed abuse, with the claimants and he sexually abused their own children. The claimants only found out afterwards. Did the claimants need to be at the event or the immediate aftermath? The House of Lords said that it was difficult to say that someone of reasonable fortitude would not be affected by these events as they had unwittingly contributed to the abuse happening. The claimants had an arguable case.

More recently in *Taylor v A Novo Ltd* [2013] EWCA Civ 194 the claimant's mother was injured at work due to her employer's negligence. Three weeks later she was at home recovering when she collapsed and died. The claimant, her daughter, witnessed her mother dying and suffered post-traumatic stress disorder. She sued the employer as a secondary victim. The Court of Appeal said that the claimant had to show physical proximity to the event, which was the accident at work not the death of her mother. The claimant did not see the accident and her claim failed. If her claim was allowed it would mean that even if her mother died from her injuries years after the accident the daughter would be able to claim. This would be stretching the concept of 'immediate aftermath' too far.

## The means by which the shock was caused
The claimant must see or hear the event or the immediate aftermath with their own unaided senses. It is not sufficient if someone is told about the event by a third party. Neither is it sufficiently proximate to see the events on television. Even if it was a live broadcast the Broadcasting Code of Ethics forbids showing recognisable individuals. The claims by those who watched the Hillsborough events live on television therefore failed. The House of Lords left open the possibility of a claim if a disaster was shown live on television. In *Alcock* in the Court of Appeal Nolan LJ gave the example of a hot air balloon up in the air and shown live on television when it bursts into flames. If the relatives of the people in the balloon suffered psychiatric harm they would be able to claim.

The claimant must also show that they suffered a sudden shock which caused the psychiatric harm. Suffering psychiatric harm as a result of witnessing something over a period of time would not satisfy this requirement for a sudden shock. An example of this is seen in *Sion v Hampstead Health Authority* [1994] 5 Med LR 170 in which due to the defendant's negligence the claimant's son was injured in a motorbike accident. The claimant sat at his son's bedside in hospital for two weeks watching him die and suffered psychiatric harm. It was held by the Court of Appeal that the claimant did not suffer a 'sudden shock' but developed his illness as a result of watching his son's deterioration over a period of time. The defendant was not liable.

| *Walters v North Glamorgan NHS Trust* [2002] **EWCA Civ 1792** | A ten month old baby was taken to hospital in South Wales. The hospital failed to diagnose acute hepatitis and the baby suffered an epileptic fit. The mother was staying in the same room and saw blood coming out of the baby's mouth. The hospital told her the baby had not suffered brain damage. The mother was then told that the baby would have to be transferred to a London hospital for a liver transplant. The mother followed the ambulance to London. The baby was put on a life support machine and the next day it was switched off. The mother was present during all this time and suffered psychiatric harm. | The Court of Appeal said that although the things that happened were over a period of 36 hours they could be treated as one 'event'. The claimant was present throughout this time and was entitled to damages. |

## Common Pitfall

When answering questions on psychiatric harm the first issue to decide is whether the claimant is a primary or secondary victim as this will dictate which rules you apply.

Sometimes deliberately it may not be clear from the question and you may need to consider both sets of rules as alternatives.

## Rescuers

If a rescuer suffers psychiatric harm can they make a successful claim? This question was addressed in another case arising from the Hillsborough disaster. In *White v Chief Constable of South Yorkshire* [1998] 1 All ER 1 the claimants were all police officers who had some role at Hillsborough and suffered psychiatric harm. Some were at the ground and some were at the mortuary but none were in any danger of physical harm. The House of Lords said that rescuers did not have a special position and had to follow the normal rules for primary and secondary victims. They could not establish that they had a close relationship of love and affection with the victims and their claims failed. Lord Hoffmann said that as a matter of policy it would be unacceptable to allow the claims by police officers when all the claims by relatives in *Alcock* had failed. The decision was by a 3/2 majority and dissenting judgments were given by Lord Goff and Lord Griffiths.

In *Chadwick v British Railways Board* [1967] 1 WLR 912 the claimant lived near a railway line. After two trains collided he went to help working in the wrecked carriages and as a result suffered psychiatric harm. He was awarded compensation. Although this decision seems to contradict *White* it can be distinguished by the fact that the claimant was in physical danger of the carriages collapsing. Following the decision in *White* a rescuer must establish that they are a primary victim or they meet the requirements for a secondary victim in order to claim.

## Up for Debate

Many people have argued that the time has come to reform the law on psychiatric harm. Read the article, 'More Than a By-Stander' by R Hewitt, NLJ, 2015 and, in the light of that, consider how the law should be reformed.

## Damage to property

A novel question is what if the claimant suffers psychiatric harm not as the result of seeing injury to someone but as the result of seeing damage to property. In *Attia v British Gas* [1987] 3 All ER 455 the defendants were installing central heating in the claimant's house. The claimant went out and when she returned she found her house on fire due to the defendant's negligence. She suffered psychiatric harm. The Court of Appeal asked the question whether a reasonable house owner seeing this event would suffer psychiatric harm at the loss of their home. They said that there was an arguable case.

# Putting it into practice

Read the question below and attempt an outline answer.

Lisa owns her own haulage business. She was driving her lorry across a bridge over a river while answering a call on her mobile phone. This distracted her and the lorry crashed into the side of the bridge and Lisa was badly injured.

Mary, who was walking across the bridge at the time of the accident, climbed into the badly damaged lorry to help Lisa. In doing so Mary suffered cuts and bruises and as a result of seeing the accident suffered post-traumatic stress disorder.

Lisa's partner Nadia was at home but she saw the accident on television and recognised the lorry. Nadia suffered severe shock and needed medication from her doctor.

The bridge, which is owned by Wessex Council, was also damaged and had to be closed for two weeks. Buses operated by Wessex Council had to be diverted to another bridge several miles further upstream which meant that Wessex Council had extra expenses for petrol and staff wages.

Olga owns a restaurant on the far side of the bridge from the town centre. While the bridge was closed her profits fell by 60%.

Olga's husband Pete was buying a house for £1 million. He applied to the Apollo Building Society for a mortgage and they instructed Ron, a surveyor, to carry out a survey. Ron sent his report to the building society stating that the house was in good condition. The building society emailed the report to Pete but advised him to have his own survey. Pete read the report and then bought the house. Shortly after moving in he found that the house was riddled with woodworm and it will cost £100,000 to remedy the problem. Ron had failed to notice the woodworm.

**Advise Mary, Nadia, Wessex Council, Olga and Pete of the claims they may make, if any, in negligence.**

## Outline answer – psychiatric injury, primary and secondary victims; economic loss including consequential economic loss; negligent mis-statement

❖ *Mary v Lisa*

   ❖ Negligence: duty of care, *Caparo* test, foreseeability, proximity, just and reasonableness; duty to rescuers.
   ❖ Breach of duty: *Bolam*, would a reasonable lorry driver answer their phone?
   ❖ Causation: 'but for' test, *Barnett v Chelsea & Kensington HMC* [1969] 1 QB 428, would Mary have suffered harm but for Lisa's negligence? No.
   ❖ Mary has suffered physical harm and post-traumatic stress disorder, a recognised psychiatric injury; Mary is a primary victim; but as she has suffered a physical injury and psychiatric harm she can claim for both, *Victorian Railways v Coultas*.

❖ *Nadia v Lisa*

  ❖ Nadia suffers severe shock; does this amount to a recognised psychiatric injury? If not she cannot claim.
  ❖ But consider if it is a recognised injury; Nadia is a secondary victim as she suffers by what she sees.
  ❖ Requirements from *Alcock*; relationship of love and affection, Nadia would have to prove such a relationship with Lisa unless they are married or in a civil partnership; proximity to accident, Nadia is not proximate; must see accident own senses, seeing on television does not satisfy this; if it was live there could be a claim; even though no individuals should be shown Nadia recognises the lorry; but unlikely to succeed here.

❖ *Wessex Council v Lisa*

  ❖ Negligence: the bridge: duty of care, *Caparo* test; foreseeability, proximity, just and reasonableness; duty owed to property owners by the road.
  ❖ Breach: *Bolam* test, the reasonable lorry driver.
  ❖ Causation: 'but for' test, damage to bridge would not have happened but for Lisa's negligence. Council can claim for the physical damage to the bridge.
  ❖ Diverting the buses: cannot claim for pure economic loss, but diverting buses is consequential economic loss resulting from physical damage to the bridge, *Spartan Steel v Martin*; can claim for the extra costs.

❖ *Olga v Lisa*

  ❖ Negligence: consider if a duty of care is owed to Olga; it may be if the restaurant is nearby; breach of duty.
  ❖ Causation: even though the 'but for' test is passed under the test of legal causation the damage could be too remote, *The Wagon Mound (No 1)* [1961] AC 388. Even if this test was met the claim is for pure economic loss and cannot be claimed, *Weller v Foot and Mouth Institute*.

❖ *Pete v Ron*

  ❖ Negligence: negligent mis-statement; *Hedley Byrne v Heller*, must be a special relationship; assumption of responsibility; and reasonable reliance.
  ❖ Ron will know that Pete may rely on the report to show a relationship.
  ❖ Ron could be seen as assuming responsibility as in *Merret v Babb*.
  ❖ Proving reasonable reliance is more difficult; was it reasonable for Pete to rely on the report given the price of the house?
  ❖ Also he was told by the building society to have his own survey. In *Smith v Bush* the buyer relied on the surveyor's report but Pete's case can be distinguished given the cost of the house and the advice; he would not be able to claim.

# Table of key cases referred to in this chapter

| Key case | Area of law | Principle |
|---|---|---|
| *Alcock v Chief Constable of South Yorkshire* [1992] 4 All ER 907 | Relatives of the victims of Hillsborough sued for psychiatric harm. All the claims failed. | Secondary victims must prove love and affection, proximity to accident or aftermath and see with own senses. |
| *Chaudry v Prabhakar* [1989] 3 All ER 718 | Negligent advice given by a friend that a car had not been in an accident. Court of Appeal said it was a negligent mis-statement. | Even a statement given by a friend may lead to liability for negligent mis-statement if there is reliance. |
| *Goodwill v BPAS* [1996] 2 All ER 161 | A negligent mis-statement made to one person that they did not need to use contraception but relied on by a third party who became pregnant; was not negligent mis-statement. | Claimant needs to show that the defendant assumed responsibility and knew the advice would be acted on without an independent check. |
| *Hedley Byrne v Heller* [1964] AC 465 | A negligent statement which is relied on and causes economic loss can create liability. | To claim for negligent mis-statement must show a special relationship, assumption of responsibility and reasonable reliance. |
| *Murphy v Brentwood District Council* [1990] 1 AC 398 | The walls of a house built on a negligently checked concrete raft began to crack and house fell in value. | The cost of fixing this was pure economic loss and could not be claimed in tort. *Anns* overruled. |
| *Smith v Bush* [1989] 2 All ER 514 | A negligent survey report given to the building society and shown to the mortgagor, contained an exclusion clause. Surveyor liable as owed a duty to mortgagor. | Duty can be owed by third party. The exclusion clause was unreasonable and invalid. |
| *Spartan Steel v Martin* [1973] 1 QB 27 | A claim for economic loss when the electricity to a steel mill was cut. | A claim could be made for consequential economic loss but not for pure economic loss. |

| | | |
|---|---|---|
| *Walters v North Glamorgan NHS Trust* [2002] EWCA Civ 1792 | A claim for psychiatric harm arising from the death of a baby. Mother present during events over 36 hours. | Everything which happened over that period was treated as one 'event' because the claimant was there and it counted as a sudden shock. |

@ Visit the book's companion website to test your knowledge

❖ Resources include a subject map, revision tip podcasts, downloadable diagrams, MCQ quizzes for each chapter and a flashcard glossary

❖ www.routledge.com/cw/optimizelawrevision

# 5 Nuisance and Rylands v Fletcher

## Revision objectives

**Understand the law**

- Can you define private nuisance, public nuisance and statutory nuisance?
- Can you distinguish between physical damage to land and interference with enjoyment of land?
- Can you outline the factors used to determine if there is interference with enjoyment of land?
- Can you explain the distinctions between private and public nuisance?
- Can you identify the requirements to claim under *Rylands v Fletcher*?

**Remember the details**

- Can you explain, using cases, the factors used to determine whether an act is a private nuisance?
- Can you explain, using examples, who can be sued for private nuisance?
- Can you explain the defences to private nuisance and whether they will be successful?
- Can you explain when a claim may be made in the tort of public nuisance?
- Can you explain the problems of non-natural use and forseeability in claims under *Rylands v Fletcher*?

**Reflect critically on areas of debate**

- Can you identify the differences between private nuisance and the other torts of *Rylands v Fletcher*, negligence and trespass to land?
- Can you comment on whether the requirement of foreseeability makes nuisance more like negligence?
- Can you comment on whether the courts have set out clear guidance to determine if the use of land is non-natural under *Rylands v Fletcher*?

**Contextualise**

- Do you understand how a balance has to be struck between landowners in applying the test of reasonableness to establish private nuisance?
- Do you understand which remedies are appropriate to given facts?
- Do you appreciate that action for public nuisance and *Rylands v Fletcher* may also be possible in addition to private nuisance?

**Apply your skills and knowledge**

- Can you analyse a set of facts and reach a reasoned conclusion on which actions are available to the claimant?
- Can you answer the question at the end of this chapter?

# Chapter Map

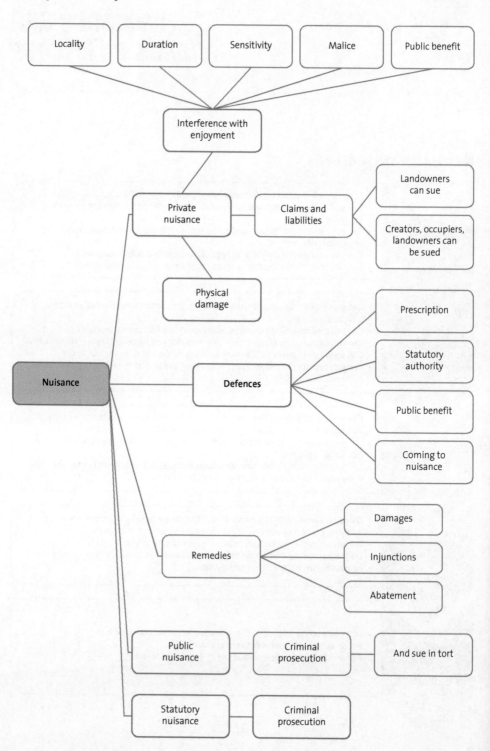

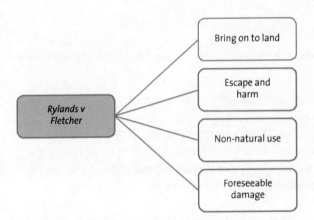

# Introduction

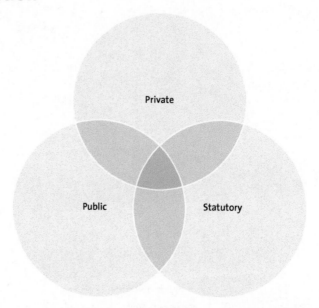

There are three types of nuisance; private nuisance, public nuisance and statutory nuisance.

❖ Private nuisance protects a person's ownership of land and if this is interfered with the owner can sue in tort.
❖ Public nuisance protects the public who have certain rights which are not connected with the ownership of land, for example, the right to walk along a street. If someone interferes with this right it is a criminal offence and they can be prosecuted. An individual who is affected more than the public generally can also sue in tort.
❖ A number of statutes create offences which are statutory nuisances which are criminal offences and prosecutions can be brought by local authorities, for example, under the Environmental Protection Act 1990.

# Private nuisance

## Definition

A private nuisance is an unlawful act, indirectly causing physical injury to land or interfering with enjoyment of or interests in land and which is unreasonable in all the circumstances.

Private nuisance is not actionable *per se* (in itself) and the claimant needs to prove actual damage. An indirect act means that the harm is a side effect of the act rather than the direct result. An example would be smoke from a bonfire going on to a neighbour's land. In contrast to this throwing a stone at the neighbour's greenhouse, would be a direct act and a trespass to land.

Private nuisance aims to balance the rights of neighbouring landowners to use their own land without unreasonably affecting one another.

The law distinguishes between various types of nuisance

## Physical injury

The claimant must suffer a material injury which means physical damage to property. With a claim for physical damage strictly the test of reasonableness applies. However, in practice the courts pay more attention to the factor of sensitivity.

---

### Case precedent – *St Helens Smelting Co v Tipping* (1865) 11 HL Cas 642

**Facts:** The claimant lived in an industrial area and fumes from the defendant's copper smelting works damaged trees growing on the claimant's land.

**Principle:** The House of Lords held that the claimant had proved physical damage to land and the defendant was liable in nuisance. The fact it was in an industrial area was irrelevant if there was physical damage to land.

**Application:** If a claimant establishes physical damage to land or something attached to the land that is sufficient for a claim in nuisance. This also includes property on the land (see *Halsey v Esso Petroleum* [1961] page 94).

An important qualification on claims for physical damage was set out in *Northum-brian Water Ltd v Sir Robert McAlpine Ltd* [2014] EWCA Civ 685. The claimant sued in nuisance after concrete from the defendant's building site went down an old drain and damaged the claimant's sewer pipe. The Court of Appeal held that following the *Cambridge Water Company Ltd v Eastern Counties Leather plc* [1994] 2 WLR 53 case foreseeability of the type of harm was necessary. Here no one knew about the old drain which was hundreds of years old and it could only be found by searching old maps. This damage was not foreseeable and the claim in nuisance failed.

## Interference with enjoyment of land

The law of nuisance protects a wide range of interests of the owners of land, for example, noise, smoke, smells and a brothel in a residential street, *Thompson-Schwab v Costaki* [1956] 1 All ER 652. New interests may be recognised from time to time. In *Hunter v Canary Wharf* [1997] 2 All ER 246 the House of Lords ruled that interference with television reception by a tall building was not a nuisance. The question remains open whether something else interfering with television reception could be a nuisance.

### Up for Debate

Should the law of nuisance now recognise the right to receive television signals or the internet?

An action will only be a nuisance if in all the circumstances it is unreasonable. In determining whether an action is unreasonable the courts take a number of factors into account if they are relevant to the particular case. The courts are not limited to these factors and any other relevant matters may be taken into account.

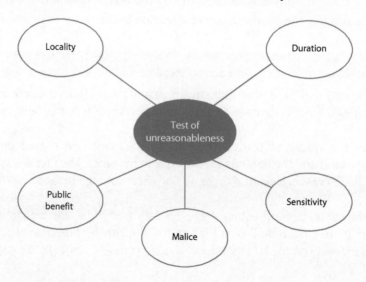

## Locality

The nature of the area is taken into account in deciding if the act is unreasonable. The classic example is *Sturges v Bridgman* (1879) in which Thesiger LJ stated, 'what would be a nuisance in Belgrave Square would not necessarily be so in Bermondsey'.

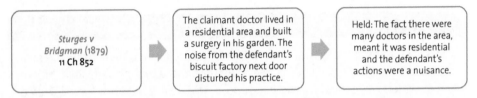

| | | |
|---|---|---|
| *Sturges v Bridgman* (1879) 11 Ch 852 | The claimant doctor lived in a residential area and built a surgery in his garden. The noise from the defendant's biscuit factory next door disturbed his practice. | Held: The fact there were many doctors in the area, meant it was residential and the defendant's actions were a nuisance. |

The character of an area can change and this will have an effect on deciding if an activity is a nuisance. This was seen in *Gillingham Borough Council v Medway Dock Co* [1992] 3 WLR 449 in which the council gave planning permission to change a naval docks into a commercial port which operated 24 hours a day. Some years later the council wanted to restrict traffic because local residents had complained about the noise. The court said that the nature of the area had changed and the noise was not a nuisance. In *Coventry v Lawrence* [2014] UKSC 13 the Supreme Court stated that the grant of planning permission, in itself, could not change the nature of the area, although it was one factor to take into account in deciding if there was a nuisance.

### Aim Higher

Questions on nuisance may be essay questions rather than problem questions. Essay questions usually involve some explanation and comment on the law or the effect of an important recent case. One such case is *Coventry v Lawrence* [2014] in which the Supreme Court made important statements about locality, the effect of planning permission and the remedies available.

Read the following article, 'Making a Noise' by Andrew Francis, 2014, 164 NLJ 15 and assess the impact of the decision on private nuisance.

## Duration

How long the interference goes on for is relevant in deciding if it is a nuisance. The longer an activity goes on the more likely it will be a nuisance. But something happening for a short time can also be a nuisance. In *Andreae v Selfridge* (1938) Ch 1 noise and dust from building work causing the loss of one night's sleep was held to be a nuisance because it could easily have been prevented. In *Crown River Cruises v Kimbolton* [1996] 2 Lloyd's Rep 533 the defendant's fireworks display lasted less than 20 minutes but the fireworks landed on the claimant's boat on the River Thames causing physical damage. This was held to be a nuisance.

There is no requirement that an action has to be continuous to be a nuisance.

## Sensitivity

The defendant's action must be something which would affect an ordinary person or ordinary property. If someone or something is abnormally sensitive they cannot claim in nuisance.

---

### Case precedent – *Robinson v Kilvert* (1889) 41 ChD 88

**Facts:** The defendant manufactured boxes in a cellar and heat from the processes reached 80 °F (27 °C). The heat damaged the claimant's sensitive brown paper which was stored on the floor above. The heat would not have affected ordinary paper.

**Principle:** The Court of Appeal held that the defendant was not liable because the defendant's activities would not have affected the ordinary use of property.

**Application:** The Court of Appeal have questioned the use of the factor of sensitivity in *Network Rail v Morris* [2004] EWCA Civ 172 in which both parties had sensitive equipment. The court relied on a test of foreseeability and said that it was not foreseeable that NR's signalling equipment would affect M's recording equipment 80 metres away and M's claim in nuisance failed.

---

However, if the defendant's activities would have damaged ordinary property then a claim can be made for sensitive property. This situation arose in *McKinnon Industries v Walker* [1951] 3 DLR 577 where gas from the defendant's factory damaged the claimant's delicate flowers. It was held that as the gas would have damaged ordinary flowers the defendant was liable in nuisance for the delicate flowers.

## Malice

In determining whether an action is unreasonable the courts take into account the defendant's intentions. If the defendant acts in a malicious way their actions can be found to be a nuisance. This is illustrated by the following case.

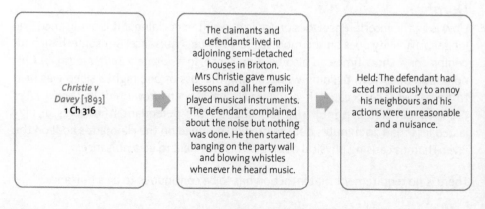

*Christie v Davey* [1893] 1 Ch 316

The claimants and defendants lived in adjoining semi-detached houses in Brixton. Mrs Christie gave music lessons and all her family played musical instruments. The defendant complained about the noise but nothing was done. He then started banging on the party wall and blowing whistles whenever he heard music.

Held: The defendant had acted maliciously to annoy his neighbours and his actions were unreasonable and a nuisance.

However, an act done with malice will not necessarily make the act a nuisance. In *Bradford Corporation v Pickles* [1895] AC 587 the defendant wanted the corporation to buy his land. He deliberately stopped water flowing through his land going into the corporation's reservoir further down the hill. The corporation claimed this was a nuisance and wanted an injunction to stop the defendant's actions. It was held that as the defendant had a lawful right to use such water his malice was irrelevant and his action was not a nuisance.

## Public benefit

If an action is a benefit to the public it may be found to be reasonable and not to be a nuisance. It is difficult to establish that an action is such a benefit to the public that it justifies creating a nuisance, for example, *Adams v Ursell* [1913].

### Example

If someone lives next to a fire station and complains about the noise of fire engines going in and out at all hours this would be seen as a public benefit and not a nuisance.

### Case precedent – *Adams v Ursell* [1913] 1 Ch 269

**Facts:** The defendants started a fish and chip shop in a residential street. The claimants lived next door and they complained about the 'fog or steam' which filled their house. The defendants argued that they provided a benefit for poor people.

**Principle:** It was held that nevertheless it was still a nuisance and an injunction was granted to stop the defendants running the shop.

**Application:** This decision shows how difficult it is to establish public benefit. However, it is a factor taken into account when deciding on the remedies and may result in damages being awarded even if an injunction is refused. See *Dennis v MOD* [2003] EWHC 793 (QB) under Nuisance and human rights on page 91.

### Common Pitfall

Sometimes the factors for the test of reasonableness are overlooked and students simply make a general comment that an act is unreasonable. An alternative approach is to put in all the factors whether they are relevant or not.

The best practice is to select those which are relevant and apply them.

## Interference with interests in land

Private nuisance also protects certain rights which a landowner may have. Examples include a right of support of their land from neighbouring land, a right to light and a right of way over someone else's land. Interference with such rights is a private nuisance.

## Natural condition of the land

A landowner was not originally liable for a nuisance caused by the natural condition of their land or for an act of nature, for example, lightning causing a fire which spread to neighbouring land. The law was changed by the following case.

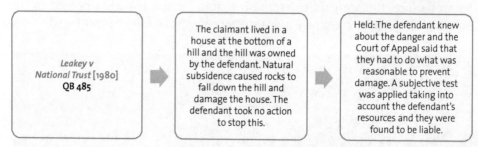

*Leakey v National Trust* [1980] QB 485

The claimant lived in a house at the bottom of a hill and the hill was owned by the defendant. Natural subsidence caused rocks to fall down the hill and damage the house. The defendant took no action to stop this.

Held: The defendant knew about the danger and the Court of Appeal said that they had to do what was reasonable to prevent damage. A subjective test was applied taking into account the defendant's resources and they were found to be liable.

The subjective test was applied in *Holbeck Hall Hotel v Scarborough Council* [2000] 2 All ER 705. The claimant's hotel was built overlooking the sea, on cliffs owned by the defendant council. The cliffs were being eroded by the sea and eventually the hotel fell into the sea. The court said that if a landowner knows about a nuisance they have a duty to prevent foreseeable damage. In this case the extent of the damage was not foreseeable without an expensive geological survey. There was no duty to have such a survey and the defendant was not liable in nuisance.

## Who can sue?

Private nuisance protects someone's interest in land. To be able to sue the claimant needs a proprietary interest in land, for example, they are a landowner or a tenant.

### Case precedent – *Malone v Laskey* [1907] 2 KB 141

**Facts:** Mrs Malone lived in a house with her husband but the tenancy was in his name. She was sitting on the toilet when due to vibrations from next door the toilet cistern fell on her and she was injured.

**Principle:** The Court of Appeal held that her claim in nuisance failed because she did not have an interest in land, she was merely a licensee of the land.

**Application:** The result of this decision is that anyone who does not have an interest in land cannot sue in private nuisance. This includes lodgers, who do not have exclusive possession, guests and children of the landowner.

The House of Lords confirmed in *Hunter v Canary Wharf* [1997] that nuisance only protects rights in land and does not extend to those living in a property. A number of people complained that Canary Wharf Tower interfered with their television reception. They included owners of property, spouses, children and lodgers. Only someone with a proprietary interest in land had a right to sue. The court also said that claims for personal injury could not be made in nuisance, but should be made in negligence.

## Common Pitfall

When identifying if someone has a claim in nuisance remember to ask if they have an interest in land. A child cannot claim if they have no interest in land (*Hunter v Canary Wharf* [1997]).

## Who can be sued?

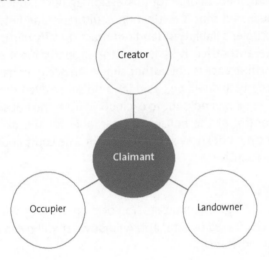

### *Creator*
Anyone who creates a nuisance may be sued, for example, a tenant of a property who frequently holds noisy parties late at night.

### *Occupier*
An occupier of land will be liable for any nuisance which they cause or which is caused by someone they control or by a previous occupier or by the act of a trespasser (third party). The occupier must adopt or continue the nuisance. This is illustrated in the following case.

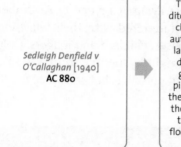

| *Sedleigh Denfield v O'Callaghan* [1940] **AC 880** | The defendants owned a ditch on the border with the claimant's land. The local authority trespassed on the land and laid a pipe in the ditch but forgot to put a grid over the end of the pipe. The defendants used the pipe to drain water from their land. Three years later the pipe blocked up and flooded the claimant's land. | The House of Lords held that the defendants had adopted and continued the nuisance by using the pipe. They were therefore liable to the claimants. |

In *Cocking v Eacott and another* [2016] EWCA Civ 140 W owned a terraced house which she let her daughter, E, live in rent free as a licensee making W the licensor. E fell out with her next door neighbours, the claimants, who complained about E's dog barking and E's abusive shouting. When W received a letter from the claimant's solicitors she argued that a landlord was not liable for a nuisance created by a tenant. W also obtained an order of possession against E but did not enforce it. The Court of Appeal said that a distinction could be made between a landlord's liability and an occupier's liability. A landlord must directly participate in the nuisance or must have authorised it by letting the property for that purpose. Doing nothing to stop the nuisance is not authorising it. An occupier has control and possession of the property and will be liable for a nuisance even though the occupier did not create it. Here E had no right to exclude W from the house and W had both possession and control of the house. W was liable for the barking but not the shouting which she did not know about until later. The court applied *Sedleigh Denfield v O'Callaghan* [1940].

## Landowner

When a landowner has given up possession of property they will not generally be liable for a nuisance created by a tenant. A landowner will be liable for a nuisance in the following circumstances:

| Landowner knows the purpose he lets the land for is a nuisance | The nuisance exists when he lets the land |

This can be illustrated in *Tetley v Chitty* [1986] 1 All ER 663 where the local authority let land in a residential area to the defendant to be used for go-karting. The court held that letting the land for go-karting meant noise was inevitable and the council was liable. Similarly in *Lippiatt v South Gloucestershire County Council* [1999] 4 All ER 149 the council allowed travellers to stay on council land. The travellers trespassed on the claimant's land and left rubbish. The council knew about these acts and had the power to remove the travellers. The council were held liable for nuisance.

# Nuisance and human rights

In addition to a claim in nuisance a claim may be made under Article 8(1) of the European Convention on Human Rights for interference with private and family life. The Human Rights Act 1998 only applies to public bodies so a claim could also be made under Article 8 if a public body is causing a nuisance.

There is no need to have an interest in land to bring a claim under Article 8.

The right under Article 8 is a qualified right and under 8(2) it may be restricted for the protection of others or in the public interest.

---

**Case precedent – *Dennis v Ministry of Defence* [2003] EWHC 793 (QB)**

**Facts:** The claimant lived near an RAF base and was affected by the frequent noise of jets flying low over his house. He claimed nuisance and breach of Article 8.

**Principle:** The court held that this did amount to a nuisance. However, under Article 8 a balance had to be maintained between the rights of the landowner and the public benefit and national security. The court said that it would be a breach of Article 8 but there was no need to rely on Article 8 because it did not add to the nuisance claim. The claimant was awarded damages for nuisance but an injunction to stop the base operating was refused.

**Application:** It is difficult to establish a claim under Article 8 although it could be used by someone who does not have an interest in land. The decision means that the rights of the claimant can be limited to damages in some circumstances.

---

# Defences

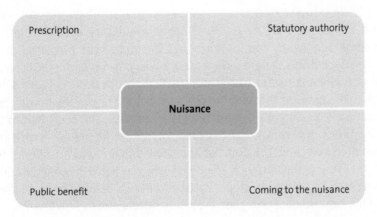

| Prescription | Statutory authority |
|---|---|
| | Nuisance | |
| Public benefit | Coming to the nuisance |

A number of defences may be used in nuisance. They include the general defences of consent and contributory negligence. The defences of prescription and statutory authority have been used successfully but those of public benefit and that the claimant came to the nuisance have not been successful.

## Prescription

If the defendant commits a private nuisance for over 20 years they will acquire a legal right to commit that nuisance by prescription, if the claimant has not objected during that time. In *Sturges v Bridgman* (1879) the defendant had been making biscuits for over 20 years but the nuisance did not start until the doctor built his surgery. As a result the defendant did not acquire a prescriptive right to make noise and the defence failed.

## Statutory authority

A statute may give power to a Government minister or local authority to carry out a particular activity. If this activity causes a nuisance the question arises whether the nuisance is authorised under the statute. If the statute expressly provides that it is that will be a defence. If the statute does not specifically provide then the statute will have to be interpreted to see if it covers the nuisance.

*Allen v Gulf Oil* [1981] 1 All ER 353

A statute gave the defendant power to build an oil refinery but not to operate it. The refinery was built and started operating and local residents complained about the noise and the smell.

Held: Parliament must have intended that the refinery could be operated. Anything which was an inevitable result of operating was not a nuisance. The claimant's case failed.

## Public benefit

The defence of public benefit has been argued in many cases but has not been successful. This was seen in *Adams v Ursell* [1913] the fish and chip shop and in *Dennis v MOD* [2003] the RAF base.

## Coming to the nuisance

Defendants also argue that they are not liable in nuisance because the claimant chose to come and live by the nuisance and therefore have consented to it. The courts have rejected this defence. The defence was put forward in *Miller v Jackson* [1977] QB 966 where a cricket club had played cricket for over 70 years. A housing estate was then built next to it and the claimant bought one of the houses. He complained that balls landing in the garden were a nuisance. The court had to balance the public interest in playing cricket against the private interest of the claimant to protect his interest in land. The Court of Appeal held that it was no defence that the claimant had come to the nuisance. The defendant was liable in nuisance and had to pay damages. An injunction to stop playing cricket was refused because the public interest in playing cricket outweighed the private interest of the landowner.

# Remedies

| Damages | Injunction | Abatement |
|---|---|---|
| • The claimant must prove damage to land or interference with enjoyment of land.<br>• Can claim for damage to goods (chattels) on the land.<br>• Can claim for economic loss which results from the damage to land.<br>• Cannot claim for personal injury. | • An injunction is a court order telling someone to stop doing a particular act.<br>• It is an equitable remedy and it is up to the court's discretion whether to grant it.<br>• In *Kennaway v Thompson* [1980] 3 All ER 329 the claimant's house overlooked a lake. The court granted an injunction restricting the times power boat racing could take place on the lake. | • A claimant affected by a nuisance has the right to stop (or abate) the nuisance.<br>• A good example is if the branch of a tree grows over the claimant's garden, the claimant can chop it off. The branch remains the property of the neighbour.<br>• A claimant using this remedy must be careful not to trespass on their neighbour's land. |

# Public nuisance

A public nuisance is a crime and the person responsible for it can be prosecuted. In *Attorney General v PYA Quarries Ltd* [1957] 2 QB 169 Romer LJ defined public nuisance as an act:

> 'which materially affects the reasonable comfort and convenience of life of a class of Her Majesty's subjects.'

Lord Denning said that a public nuisance was something so widespread that it would not be reasonable to expect one person to take action to stop it.

A public nuisance covers a wide range of actions, for example, obstructing a public highway, selling food which is unfit for human consumption and being naked in public.

The act must affect the public generally or a class of the public. How many people constitute a 'class' is a question of fact in each case. In *R v Rimmington* [2005] UKHL 63 the defendant sent over 500 racially abusive letters to individual people. The House of Lords said that the letters only affected those private individuals and not a 'class' of persons, therefore it was not a public nuisance.

**Case precedent – *Halsey v Esso Petroleum Co Ltd* [1961] 2 All ER 145**

**Facts:** The claimant lived in Fulham opposite the defendant's oil depot. He complained about: (i) acid smuts damaging the washing on the line; (ii) the smell of oil; (iii) noise from the boilers in the depot; (iv) noise from lorries in the depot; (v) acid smuts damaging his car on the road; and (vi) noise from lorries going into the depot.

**Principle:** The court said that noise at night was particularly significant as most people were in bed. It was held that (i)–(iv) were private nuisances and (v) and (vi) were public nuisances.

**Application:** This decision shows the distinction between private and public nuisance. One act can be both private and public nuisance.

## Suing in tort for a public nuisance

An individual who can show that they have suffered 'special' damage over and above that suffered by the public or a class of the public may sue in the tort of public nuisance. The special or particular damage includes physical damage to property, personal injury and economic or financial loss. The reason for this rule is to stop every individual affected by the public nuisance suing the defendant.

The claimant does not need an interest in land to sue in the tort of public nuisance. An example of such a claim is *Tate & Lyle Ltd v GLC* [1983] 1 All ER 1159. The defendant council built a ferry terminal in the River Thames which caused the river to silt up. The court held that this interfered with the right of navigation and it was a public nuisance. Although the claimant did not suffer any damage to their property they had to dredge the river around their own jetty and suffered particular damage.

If an individual cannot show they have suffered particular damage they can ask the Attorney General for permission to start civil proceedings known as a relator action. This may result in the claimant obtaining an injunction to stop the nuisance.

## Common Pitfall

If a problem question asks about claims in 'private nuisance' the answer should be limited to that. If a question asks for liability in 'nuisance' then the alternative of public nuisance should be considered. The advantages of taking action in public nuisance are that there is no need for an interest in land and a claim may be made for personal injury.

## Distinctions between private and public nuisance

| Private nuisance | Public nuisance |
|---|---|
| Only a tort | Crime and a tort |
| Must have an interest in land to sue | No need for an interest in land |
| Cannot claim for personal injury | Can claim for personal injury |
| Defence of prescription may apply | Prescription does not apply |
| Only one person needs to be affected | Must affect the public or a class of the public |

# Statutory nuisance

A number of statutes provide that certain actions amount to a statutory nuisance. The main example is the Environmental Protection Act 1990. Under this Act certain things are classed as statutory nuisances, for example, smoke, noise and premises in a state prejudicial to health. The local authority has power to serve an abatement notice on the person responsible for the nuisance and failure to comply with the notice is a criminal offence. In *Royal Borough of Greenwich v Ogbuka Housing Ltd* [2015] EWHC 2707 (QB) residents on a housing estate complained about noise from buildings on a nearby industrial estate. The buildings were being used as a church and social club and the noise sometimes went on all night. The council served a noise abatement notice on the defendant who was later convicted for breach of the order. The council later obtained an injunction in the High Court to stop the activities.

Involving the council may be an alternative to bringing a claim in private nuisance.

# *Rylands v Fletcher* (1865) 3 H&C 774

## Introduction
A distinction is made in tort between fault liability and strict liability.

| Fault liability | Strict liability |
|---|---|
| A person is only liable if they are at fault e.g. act negligently | A person is liable even though they have not done anything wrong and are not at fault e.g. *Rylands v Fletcher* |

The rule in *Rylands v Fletcher* is based on the case and is a separate tort to nuisance. It provides that a landowner is strictly liable if something escapes from his land and causes harm to other land.

In *Rylands v Fletcher* (1865) the defendant owned a mill and engaged an independent contractor to build a reservoir for him. The contractor discovered some unused mineshafts but did not block them up. When the reservoir was filled, the water went down the mineshafts and flooded the claimant's mine. The defendant did not know about the mine shafts. It was held that the defendant was liable even though he was not to blame.

The rule in *Rylands v Fletcher* was set out by Blackburn J at first instance:

> 'the person who, for his own purposes, brings on his land and collects and keeps there anything likely to do mischief if it escapes, must keep it in at his peril; and if he does not do so, is *prima facie* answerable for all the damage which is the natural consequence of its escape.'

In order to sue under *Rylands v Fletcher* the claimant must have an interest in land.

## Requirements for liability
There are four requirements to establish liability under *Rylands v Fletcher*.

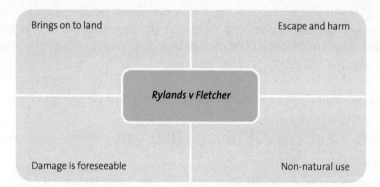

Brings on to land

Escape and harm

*Rylands v Fletcher*

Damage is foreseeable

Non-natural use

### Brings on to land
The defendant must bring something on to his land. There is no liability for something naturally on the land which escapes, for example, thistles growing naturally.

It must be something which is likely to do mischief. This includes inherently dangerous things, for example, explosives, gas, electricity, fire, a lion etc. but also normally safe things, for example, water or strips of metal foil which can do damage if they escape. In *Transco plc v Stockport Metropolitan Borough Council* [2003] UKHL 61 Lord Bingham said that it had to be shown that the defendant ought to have recognised that there was 'an exceptionally high risk of danger or mischief if there should be an escape'.

## It escapes and causes harm

There must be an escape from the defendant's land. This requirement was not fulfilled in *Read v Lyons* [1947] AC 156. The claimant was a munitions inspector who
was visiting the defendant's factory when a shell exploded and she was injured.
The defendants had not acted negligently. The House of Lords held that as there
was no escape from land the defendant was not liable under *Rylands v Fletcher*.

The escape must cause damage to property. The rule does not cover personal
injury.

## Non-natural use of land

The claimant must show that the defendant's use of land was non-natural. This
means it is not an ordinary use of land. Determining what is an ordinary use will
depend on the circumstances and the period in history and the meaning will
change over time.

### Example

Using electricity for domestic purposes is now an ordinary use of land but
would not have been in the nineteenth century.

In *Rickards v Lothian* [1913] AC 280 Lord Moulton said that the use of land must
bring increased danger to others and is not merely ordinary use or use 'for the
general benefit of the community'. However, a contrary view was expressed in
*Cambridge Water Company Ltd v Eastern Counties Leather plc* [1994] by Lord
Goff who said that storing chemicals in industrial premises was a non-natural
use of land. He added that if something was for the benefit of the community
that did not make it a natural use and therefore avoid liability under the rule.

Further guidance was given by Lord Hoffmann in *Transco plc v Stockport
Metropolitan Borough Council* [2003] who said that in deciding whether something is a non-natural use, ask if the damage was something which the occupier could reasonably be expected to have insured against. If insurance should
have been taken out it would be an ordinary use and there would be no liability. The case concerned a water pipe to the defendant's block of flats which
burst. Water escaped and washed soil away from the claimant's gas main. The
claimant sued under *Rylands v Fletcher*. The court said that the supply of water
in a pipe was a normal and ordinary use of land and therefore a natural use.
The defendant was not liable.

## Damage is foreseeable

The original rule imposed strict liability for an escape. In *Cambridge Water* [1994]
the House of Lords added the requirement that damage had to be foreseeable.

> ### Case precedent – *Cambridge Water Company Ltd v Eastern Counties Leather plc* [1994] 2 WLR 53
>
> **Facts:** The defendant used a chemical in the tanning process until 1976. Some of the chemical seeped through the concrete floor and into the claimant's borehole over one mile away contaminating the water. The contamination was not discovered until 1983 and the claimants had to drill a new borehole costing £1 million.
>
> **Principle:** The House of Lords said that to claim under *Rylands v Fletcher* it had to be proved that damage was foreseeable. When the chemical was brought on to the land the defendant could not foresee that it would damage the claimant's water supply and the defendant was not liable.
>
> **Application:** The test of foreseeability is that at the time the thing was brought on to the land the defendant had to foresee that if it escaped it would cause the type of damage suffered. Here some damage was foreseeable but not to the claimant's water supply over one mile away.

Consequently the damage must be foreseeable but the escape does not have to be foreseeable.

## Defences

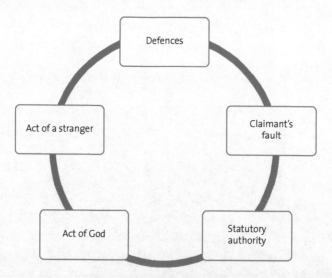

### Act of a stranger

If the escape is caused by the act of a stranger (third party) the defendant has no control over, the defendant will not be liable. If the act of the third party could have been foreseen the defence fails and the defendant is liable.

## Act of God

If the escape is caused by natural forces and could not have been foreseen this is a good defence.

## Statutory authority

A statute may provide a defence for someone carrying out high risk activities.

## Claimant's fault

If it is established that the escape is the claimant's fault, that is a good defence. In *Ponting v Noakes* [1894] 2 QB 281 the claimant's horse ate some poisonous leaves on the defendant's tree and the horse died. The defendant was not liable.

**Aim Higher**

*Rylands v Fletcher* is usually part of a problem question on nuisance.

However, it may be an essay question on its own and often takes the form of asking whether it is still needed or whether it could be abolished.

**Up for Debate**

It is important to remember the relationships between private nuisance and other torts of *Rylands v Fletcher*, negligence and trespass.

Nuisance protects a person's interest in land. It is based on a test of reasonableness which involves asking if the defendant has acted unreasonably in relation to the claimant's land. This involves a balancing exercise between the two landowners.

Negligence protects a person from injury or damage to their property. Liability is based on a test of the reasonable person and is an objective test. If the defendant does not reach that standard they are liable.

*Rylands v Fletcher* deals with isolated escapes from land and originally liability was strict. Since the *Cambridge Water* case in 1994 the damage must now be foreseeable which brings it in line with nuisance.

Trespass protects landowners from direct acts which cause damage to land. This is in contrast to nuisance which protects from indirect acts.

## Putting it into practice

Look at the scenario below and then answer the following question.

Harriet owns a terraced house in a town. She lets the house to three students Ivor, Jamil and Kim.

Liz lives next door to the left of Harriet's house. Liz complains about the noise from the students who often have parties until 3.00 am which keep Liz awake. Liz also complains that the street is frequently littered with beer cans and empty wine bottles from the parties. On one occasion when Liz was parking her car in the street one of the tyres burst on a broken wine bottle.

Molly, a professional wine taster, recently bought the terraced house to the right of Harriet's house. Her sister Nadia moved in to live with her. Ivor keeps a pet pig in his back garden and the smells invade Molly's house, make her ill and affect her sense of taste. Molly complained to Ivor about the smell but he then began lighting fires to burn the waste straw from the pig's bedding, which makes the smell even worse.

One afternoon Ivor lit a big bonfire which created clouds of smoke and burning straw. Nadia was sunbathing in the garden and some burning straw from the bonfire blew over the garden wall and burned her legs. Some of the burning straw also landed on the roof of Molly's house and damaged the roof tiles.

**Advise Liz, Molly and Nadia of any action they may take in tort.**

## Outline answer – private nuisance, public nuisance and *Rylands v Fletcher*

### Identify legal issues and define legal principles
❖ *Liz and the noise*

    ❖ Define private nuisance; an indirect act causing physical injury to land or interfering with enjoyment of land.

- ❖ The noise interferes with the enjoyment of land. The test of reasonableness applies: relevant factors – locality; in *Sturges v Bridgman* it was a residential area and the noise was a nuisance. Liz lives in a town and consider if her situation can be distinguished or is it also residential? Duration: the students hold parties often; they also go on late at night; this would suggest a nuisance.

- ❖ *Can Liz sue for private nuisance?*

  - ❖ To sue in private nuisance a person needs an interest in land; in *Malone v Laskey* Mrs Malone's claim failed because she did not have an interest in land.
  - ❖ In applying this here the point is arguable as all that is known is Liz lives next door. If she is the owner or a tenant she would be able to sue.

- ❖ *Who is liable?*

  - ❖ It could be the creators of the nuisance, the students Ivor, Jamil and Kim.
  - ❖ It could also be Harriet, the landlord. In *Tetley v Chitty* the local authority let the land for go-karting, so noise was inevitable and the local authority were liable; *Cocking v Eacott*. Consider how these could apply: does letting the house to students mean that noise is inevitable? Does Harriet know about the problems?
  - ❖ Remedies: damages; possible injunction?

- ❖ *Liz and her car tyre*

  - ❖ The car is in the street so no claim can be made for private nuisance.
  - ❖ Do the beer cans and wine bottles amount to a public nuisance? A public nuisance is an act which affects the public or a class of the public so this could be a public nuisance.
  - ❖ Liz suffers over and above the public as her car tyre is punctured and she could sue in the tort of public nuisance, *Halsey v Esso*.

- ❖ *Molly and the smell from the pigs*

  - ❖ Does the smell amount to a private nuisance? This could be interference with enjoyment of land. The test of reasonableness applies; relevant factors – locality: keeping pigs in a town? Duration: the smell is likely to be constant; sensitivity: is Molly too sensitive? In *Robinson v Kilvert* the defendant was not liable because the claimant's paper was too sensitive. It is likely that the smell of pigs would affect a normal person.
  - ❖ Molly is unlikely to be able to claim nuisance because her sense of taste is affected as nuisance only protects interests in land, *Hunter v Canary Wharf*.
  - ❖ Molly bought the house and satisfies the requirement to have an interest in land. Molly's claim will be against Ivor unless Harriet knew that he was going to keep a pig in the garden.

❖  *Molly and the roof tiles*

   ❖  This is physical injury to land, *St Helens Smelting Co v Tipping* and Molly can claim in private nuisance.

❖  *Nadia's burns*

   ❖  Briefly consider whether Nadia could claim for private nuisance. There are two difficulties. First, no claim can be made for personal injury. Second, does Nadia have a tenancy agreement with Molly or is she simply a lodger? If the latter she would not be able to claim.

   ❖  Could Nadia claim under public nuisance? It is a public nuisance only if the public or a class of the public have been affected. It is a big fire and burning straw may have affected enough for a class of people to be affected. If so Nadia has suffered more than the public and could claim for her burns. If this could not be established Nadia would not be able to claim.

   ❖  Consider if there is a possible claim under *Rylands v Fletcher*? The requirements are bringing something on to land, which escapes and causes harm, which is a non-natural use of land and the damage is foreseeable. It may be difficult to establish a bonfire is non-natural use of land.

   ❖  In any event *Rylands v Fletcher* does not cover personal injury and Nadia's claim would fail.

The answer is illustrated in brief below:

| Liz | Molly | Nadia |
|---|---|---|
| Noise: define private nuisance | Smell of pigs: private nuisance | Burns: private nuisance? |
| Apply test of reasonableness: locality and duration | Test of reasonableness: locality, duration, sensitivity | Cannot claim for personal injury; or if no interest in land |
| Needs interest in land: depends if Liz an owner or tenant | Needs interest in land; here bought house, *Malone v Laskey* [1907] | Public nuisance? Only if public or a class affected |
| Who is liable? Students or landlord | Sense of taste: cannot claim as nuisance only protects interests in land | Argument to say it is public Nadia suffers above public and can claim in tort of public nuisance |
| *Tetley v Chitty* [1986] | | *Tate & Lyle Ltd v GLC* [1983] |
| Car tyre: define public nuisance | Roof tiles: physical injury to land | *Rylands v Fletcher*: four requirements but difficult to show bonfire is non-natural use |
| Car in street | *St Helens Smelting Co v Tipping* (1865) | Cannot claim for personal injury |
| Suffers over public | Molly can claim | Nadia's claim fails |
| Liz can sue in tort of public nuisance | | |
| *Halsey v Esso* [1961] | | |

# Table of key cases referred to in this chapter

| Key case | Area of law | Principle |
|---|---|---|
| *Cambridge Water Company Ltd v Eastern Counties Leather plc* [1994] 2 WLR 53 | Escape of chemicals which leaked through the ground to a water source one mile away. Defendants not liable under *Rylands v Fletcher* as this was not foreseeable. | Important to establish that the damage is foreseeable when the thing is brought on to land. |
| *Christie v Davey* (1893) 1 Ch 316 | The neighbour of the musical family banged on wall when they played instruments. The neighbour's malice made his action a nuisance. | If someone acts out of malice that can make the act unreasonable and a nuisance. |
| *Coventry v Lawrence* [2014] UKSC 13 | The claimant moved to a house 500 metres from a stadium where car racing took place. The local authority had granted planning permission. It was held that the racing was a nuisance. | Planning permission does not of itself mean an activity is not a nuisance. It is up to the courts to decide that. |
| *Halsey v Esso Petroleum Co Ltd* [1961] 2 All ER 145 | The claimant lived near the defendant's oil depot and complained about the noise and smell. They were a private nuisance. His car parked on the road was also damaged by acid smuts and this was held to be a public nuisance. | Private nuisances affect land and claims can also be made for property on land. Public nuisance affects the wider public. |
| *Malone v Laskey* [1907] 2 KB 141 | Vibrations from next door caused toilet cistern to fall on Mrs Malone. Claim in private nuisance failed because she did not have an interest in land. | A claimant needs an interest in land to sue in nuisance. Confirmed by *Hunter v Canary Wharf* [1997]. |
| *Miller v Jackson* [1977] QB 966 | The claimant bought a house next to a cricket club and complained that balls landed in his garden. It was held that this was a nuisance. | It is not a defence that the claimant came to the nuisance and has therefore consented to it. |

| Key case | Area of law | Principle |
|---|---|---|
| *St Helens Smelting Co v Tipping* (1865) 11 HL Cas 642 | Fumes from the defendant's factory damaged trees on claimant's land. | If physical damage to land is established that is private nuisance. No need to consider nature of locality. |
| *Sturges v Bridgman* (1879) 11 Ch 852 | Noise from the defendant's biscuit factory was a nuisance to the doctor next door; it was a residential area; held to be a nuisance. | The issue of locality is important in deciding if an act interferes with the enjoyment of land. Also authority on defence of prescription if a nuisance is committed for 20 years. |
| *Tate & Lyle v GLC* [1983] 1 All ER 1159 | Defendant's ferry terminal caused a public nuisance by silting up the river. The claimant had to pay to dredge around their jetty and claimed in the tort of public nuisance as they had suffered above public. | To claim in the tort of public nuisance the claimant has to show more damage than the public have suffered. |

@ Visit the book's companion website to test your knowledge

❖ Resources include a subject map, revision tip podcasts, downloadable diagrams, MCQ quizzes for each chapter and a flashcard glossary

❖ www.routledge.com/cw/optimizelawrevision

# 6

# Trespass to the Person

## Revision objectives

### Understand the law

- Can you distinguish between a direct act and an indirect act?
- Can you define assault, battery and false imprisonment?
- Can you identify the three main defences to trespass to the person?
- Can you describe the tort of *Wilkinson v Downton*?

### Remember the details

- Can you explain the requirements to establish an assault?
- Can you explain whether an act has to be hostile in order to amount to a battery?
- Can you explain using examples from cases what must be proved to establish false imprisonment?
- Can you explain the defence of self-defence?
- Can you distinguish between a claim in trespass and a claim under *Wilkinson v Downton*?

### Reflect critically on areas of debate

- Can you explain the significance of words in assault?
- Can you identify areas of the law of trespass to the person which are unclear?
- Can you explain whether someone who is injured escaping from false imprisonment can recover compensation?

### Contextualise

- Do you understand how the relationship between assault and battery works in practice?
- Do you understand the relationship between claims in negligence and trespass and between trespass and *Wilkinson v Downton*?
- Do you understand the cases on what is a reasonable way out in false imprisonment?

### Apply your skills and knowledge

- Can you critically comment on the law of trespass?
- Can you answer the problem question at the end of this chapter?

# Chapter Map

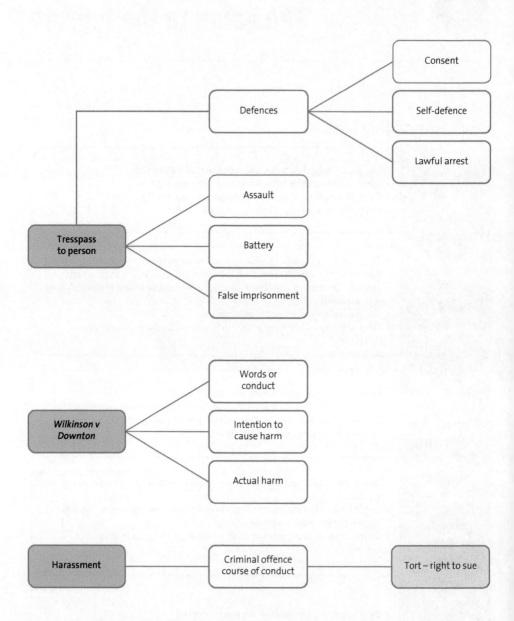

Defences
- Consent
- Self-defence
- Lawful arrest

Tresspass to person
- Assault
- Battery
- False imprisonment

Wilkinson v Downton
- Words or conduct
- Intention to cause harm
- Actual harm

Harassment — Criminal offence course of conduct — Tort – right to sue

# Introduction

This chapter will explain trespass to the person which consists of the torts of assault, battery and false imprisonment and it will also explain the tort of *Wilkinson v Downton* [1897] 2 QB 57 and the tort of harassment.

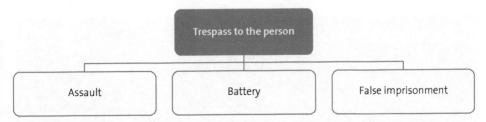

To claim for trespass the claimant must show that the act against them was a direct act.

❖ A direct act is an act which directly affects another person, for example, throwing a stick at them which hits them. A claim can then be made for trespass to the person.
❖ An indirect act is an act which affects another but not in such a direct way, for example, throwing a stick in the road which the other person trips over and is injured. In this second case they can claim for negligence rather than trespass.

In *Letang v Cooper* [1965] 1 QB 232 the claimant was sunbathing on the grass in an hotel car park when the defendant drove his car over her legs. A claim in negligence is barred after three years from when the right to sue arose under the Limitation Act 1980 but a claim in trespass may be made up to six years afterwards. As three years had passed, the claimant sued for trespass. The Court of Appeal said that if force is intentionally applied directly to another, a claim may be made in trespass. If an injury is caused unintentionally the claim is only in negligence. Here there was no intention to touch the claimant and the only claim could be in negligence but as three years had passed the claim failed.

A second distinction from negligence is that in negligence the claimant must prove that they have suffered harm. Any claim for assault, battery or false imprisonment is actionable *per se* (in itself) which means that there is no need to prove harm.

# Assault

## Definition

'An act which causes another person to apprehend the infliction of immediate, unlawful force on his person' (Goff L J in *Collins v Wilcock* [1984] 3 All ER 374).

The word 'assault' has a particular meaning in trespass which is that someone is subjected to a threat of immediate harm. An example of this is someone raising their fist to another person which would make that person believe they were about to be hit. This meaning is in contrast to the popular meaning of assault which is to hit someone.

## Common Pitfall

It is easy to mix up an assault in civil law with an assault in criminal law which is actually hitting someone.

In civil law it is simply a threat to someone which puts them in fear of being hit.

### Case precedent – Stephens v Myers (1830) 4 C&P 349

**Facts:** A group of people including the claimant and the defendant were sitting around a table at a parish meeting. Following an argument the defendant stood up, clenched his fist and moved towards the claimant. He was stopped before he reached the claimant and was not near enough to hit him.

**Principle:** It was held that the claimant had been put in fear of being hit and it was therefore an assault.

**Application:** In deciding whether the defendant believed they would be hit, the courts apply an objective test – what the reasonable person would believe rather than a subjective test – what the claimant believed.

The claimant must be put in fear of an immediate battery i.e. being hit immediately. The test to decide this is an objective test what the reasonable person would believe. In *Thomas v National Union of Mineworkers* [1985] 2 All ER 1 as working miners were being taken into the mine on a bus, a large crowd of striking miners were raising their fists and shouting threats at them. There was a police cordon between the striking miners and the bus. It was held that the miners on the bus were safe and there was no danger of an immediate battery, so no assault had been committed.

What if the defendant points a gun at the claimant? This will be an assault as the claimant will be put in fear of a battery. It will be the same even if the gun is not loaded because the claimant will not know that.

## Words

Can words alone be an assault? There are conflicting cases on this point. In *Meade's Case* (1823) 1 Lew CC 184 it was said that words were not an assault.

In *R v Wilson* [1955] 1 WLR 493 the court said that words could be an assault. In *R v Ireland* [1998] AC 147 the House of Lords said that even silent phone calls were an assault and it doubted *Meade's Case* and said that words could amount to an assault. Although *R v Ireland* is a criminal case the same rule could be followed in civil law.

Words may be relevant in deciding whether an act amounts to an assault.

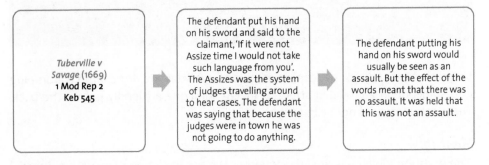

*Tuberville v Savage* (1669) 1 Mod Rep 2 Keb 545

The defendant put his hand on his sword and said to the claimant, 'If it were not Assize time I would not take such language from you'. The Assizes was the system of judges travelling around to hear cases. The defendant was saying that because the judges were in town he was not going to do anything.

The defendant putting his hand on his sword would usually be seen as an assault. But the effect of the words meant that there was no assault. It was held that this was not an assault.

# Battery

> ## Definition
>
> A battery is the application of unlawful force to another person, for example, punching someone.

There does not have to be personal contact such as touching someone with your hand. For example, throwing water, spitting or snatching someone's bag, are all examples of battery.

## Act
The defendant must commit an act. There is no need for that act to be done with force. One of the purposes of the tort of trespass is to protect a person from physical harm and another is to protect their personal integrity which means that they must be left alone.

## Direct
The touching must be the direct result of the defendant's act. The courts have interpreted directly quite widely. In *DPP v K* [1990] 1 WLR 1067 a 15 year old schoolboy put some sulphuric acid in a hand dryer at school. The next pupil used the dryer to dry his face and was badly injured. It was held that this was a direct act and a battery.

## Intention to commit the act
The defendant must intend to do the act. If the act is simply done negligently then any claim must be for negligence and not for trespass, see *Letang v Cooper* [1965] in the Introduction above. There is no need for an intention to cause harm.

## Common Pitfall

For a claim in battery the claimant does not need to prove that the defendant had an intention to harm the claimant as in criminal law but simply an intention to do the act, for example, to slap the claimant. The act must also be voluntary so if the defendant suffers from a condition which causes them to swing their arms about and they slap someone, that act is not a battery.

Some physical contact is accepted as part of everyday life, for example, bumping into someone in a crowded street or giving someone a friendly pat on the back. These actions would not be battery.

## Hostile

One question which has arisen is whether the act has to be done with a 'hostile' intent.

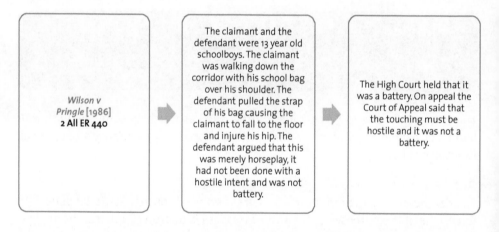

Wilson v Pringle [1986] 2 All ER 440

The claimant and the defendant were 13 year old schoolboys. The claimant was walking down the corridor with his school bag over his shoulder. The defendant pulled the strap of his bag causing the claimant to fall to the floor and injure his hip. The defendant argued that this was merely horseplay, it had not been done with a hostile intent and was not battery.

The High Court held that it was a battery. On appeal the Court of Appeal said that the touching must be hostile and it was not a battery.

The difficulty remains of deciding exactly what 'hostile' means. In *Wilson v Pringle* the court gave some examples of hostile acts like punching, stabbing and shooting but said the meaning was wider than this. The court gave the following example. In *Collins v Wilcock* [1984] W was a police officer on duty in the street. W suspected C of soliciting and tried to question her but C began to walk away. W then took hold of her arm and C scratched W. Subsequently C was convicted of assault in a criminal court. On appeal the court said that when W took hold of C's arm she was not arresting C. The act was beyond acceptable physical contact between two citizens. The act was unlawful, hostile and therefore a battery by W. C's conviction was quashed.

In *Re F* [1990] 2 AC 1 in the House of Lords Lord Goff addressed the question whether the touching had to be hostile for the purposes of battery.

'I respectfully doubt whether that is correct. A prank that gets out of hand; an overfriendly slap on the back; surgical treatment by a surgeon who mistakenly thinks the patient has consented to it – all these things may transcend the bounds of lawfulness, without being characterised as hostile. Indeed the suggested qualification is difficult to reconcile with the principle that any touching of another's body is, in the absence of a lawful excuse, capable of amounting to a battery and a trespass.'

Lord Goff made the point that if it was necessary to prove the act was hostile there would be lots of examples of acts which were not hostile but could still be seen as battery. If a surgeon operated on a patient by mistake this would not be a hostile act but should the patient have a claim for battery? Clearly the patient would have a claim.

## Transferred intent

It must be shown that the defendant intended to apply force to another person. It does not matter that the person hit was not the intended victim. The principle of 'transferred intent' from criminal law also applies in trespass. In *Livingstone v Ministry of Defence* [1984] NI 356 a soldier fired a rubber bullet at a rioter but missed and hit the claimant. It was argued that this was not a battery because the soldier did not intend to hit the claimant. It was held that the soldier was liable in battery.

Usually assault and battery will occur together, for example, someone will go up to another person, raise their fist and punch them, so the victim sees what is happening.

If someone creeps up behind the victim and punches them this will be a battery only.

# False imprisonment

## Definition

False imprisonment is a defendant intentionally stopping someone moving freely without a lawful justification.

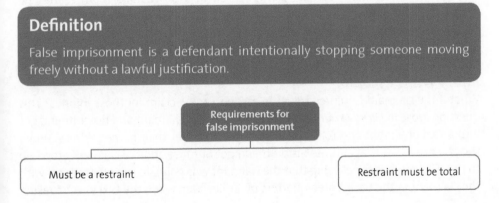

# Must be a restraint

False imprisonment is committed if there is an act which prevents the claimant moving freely. There is no requirement for the claimant to be imprisoned or physically restrained. For example, a teacher telling a pupil to wait in a room amounts to false imprisonment.

There must be an act by the defendant and an omission which leads to false imprisonment is not enough. In *Iqbal v Prison Officers Association* [2009] EWCA Civ 1312 prison officers who were on strike refused to unlock the claimant's cell. It was held that this was an omission and they were not liable for false imprisonment.

## The restraint must be total

To be false imprisonment there must be no reasonable way out.

---

### Case precedent – *Bird v Jones* (1845) 7 QB 742

**Facts:** The defendant fenced off part of the footpath on one side of Hammersmith Bridge for people to pay to watch a boat race. The claimant, who usually walked along that footpath, climbed over the fence without paying. He was stopped from walking further by two police officers and told he could go back and cross the bridge on the other side but he refused to do so.

**Principle:** It was held that he had not been totally restrained and he had a reasonable way out therefore it was not false imprisonment. The court said that a prison must have a boundary.

**Application:** The case sets out two important factors which must be applied to determine if someone has been falsely imprisoned, a 'total' restraint and no 'reasonable' way out.

---

In *Bird v Jones* the claimant had a reasonable way out even though it was not the way he wished to go. If someone was locked in a downstairs room it may be reasonable, depending on their age and health, to climb out of a window. If the room was on a higher floor it would probably not be reasonable to climb out. If the means of escape is dangerous for the claimant it is not reasonable.

## *Injury while escaping*

What if the claimant is injured trying to escape, can he claim for those injuries? This question arose in *Hicks v Young* [2015] EWHC 1144. The claimant and his girlfriend got into a taxi one night and told the defendant taxi driver their home address. When the taxi arrived at that address his girlfriend got out first and the claimant stood up to pay. The defendant believing that the claimant was going to run off drove off with the claimant in the back. Three-quarters of a mile later, when the taxi was travelling at over 20 mph the claimant jumped out. As a result he suffered brain injuries. He sued for negligence and false imprisonment. It was held that as regards the claim for false imprisonment the claimant had been unlawfully imprisoned. The court said that in trespass a person was liable to pay damages for the direct consequences of their deliberate act. Those consequences included reasonable steps taken by the claimant to end the imprisonment. However, the claimant did not act reasonably and his injuries were too remote from the imprisonment. He was, however, entitled to damages for his detention in the taxi.

## Reasonable way out

One question to determine is whether there is a reasonable way out if the defendant imposes conditions on the claimant. Compare the following similar cases.

| *Robinson v Balmain New Ferry Company* [1910] AC 295 | *Herd v Weardale Steel Co* [1915] AC 67 |
|---|---|
| The defendants operated a ferry service between Sydney and Balmain. On the Sydney side only, a turnstile was put up and a notice stated that one penny had to be paid for entrance and exit. The claimant paid a penny to go on the ferry but on finding he had to wait 20 minutes he decided to leave but refused to pay another penny. It was held by the Privy Council that the condition was reasonable to ask for payment to leave a different way. The claimant could have left on the ferry and it was not false imprisonment. | The claimant miner went down the mine for his shift. The miners believed the work they were asked to do was dangerous and asked to be taken to the surface before the end of the shift but the employers refused. It was held by the House of Lords that the claimant had voluntarily gone down the mine until the end of the shift. It was not false imprisonment. |

## Aim Higher

Reading a few cases for each topic will give you a deeper understanding of how the courts use legal principles and how each side argues their case.

See Viscount Haldane's example of the passenger on an express train in *Herd v Weardale Steel Co* [1915].

## Knowledge of imprisonment

Originally, in order to claim false imprisonment a person had to know that they had been falsely imprisoned. This was shown in *Herring v Boyle* (1834) 6 C&P 496 in which a ten year old boy was kept at boarding school during the Christmas holidays because his mother had not paid the fees. It was held that he had not been falsely imprisoned because he did not realise that he was being restrained in any way.

The case of *Herring v Boyle* (1834) was not cited to the court in *Meering v Grahame-White Aviation Co Ltd* (1919) 122 LT 44. In *Murray v Ministry of Defence* [1988] 2 All ER 521 the House of Lords said that knowledge of false imprisonment was not an essential element of the tort. It disapproved *Herring* and approved *Meering*.

*Meering v Grahame-White Aviation Co Ltd* (1919) **122 LT 44** → The claimant was suspected of theft by his employer. He was taken to a waiting room by two works policemen and agreed to stay. He was questioned for an hour but unknown to him the two works policemen stayed outside the room to stop him leaving. → The Court of Appeal said that there was no need to show that the claimant knew he was falsely imprisoned. This was false imprisonment. Atkin LJ said, 'I think a person can be imprisoned while he is asleep, drunk, unconscious or a lunatic'.

## Up for Debate

An essay question on trespass to the person could ask for a critical appraisal of the law. This would require an explanation of the rules and the important cases. But it would also require candidates to identify areas of the law which are unclear and make some comment on the problems.

Examples include determining: if a battery is 'immediate'; if words can be an assault; whether an act has to be hostile for a battery; whether a claimant needs to know that they have been falsely imprisoned; what is meant by a 'reasonable' way out.

## Defences to trespass

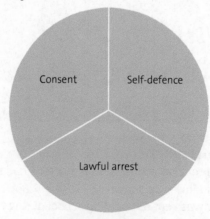

Consent

Self-defence

Lawful arrest

## Consent

If someone consents to a battery this will be a good defence. The consent may be an express consent or an implied consent. A patient will normally provide an express consent to an operation by signing a consent form. In contact sports a member of a football or hockey team will give an implied consent by playing in the game. In *Herd v Weardale Steel Co* [1915] the miner had consented to go down the mine and under his contract of employment had no right to come to the surface until the end of the shift.

## Self-defence

A person may use 'reasonable force' to defend themselves, their spouse or another person from attack. It is up to the defendant to prove that the force used was reasonable. This can be illustrated by *Lane v Holloway* [1968] 1 QB 379. The claimant, aged 64, returned from the pub and stopped outside his house to chat to a neighbour. The defendant's wife, who lived next door called out to him from her bedroom window. The claimant replied, 'Shut up you monkey faced tart'. The defendant, aged 23, appeared at the window and the claimant said, 'I want to see you on your own'. The defendant came down and approached the claimant who punched him on the shoulder. The defendant then punched the claimant once in the face. The cut needed 19 stitches. Could the defendant succeed in claiming self-defence? The Court of Appeal held that in the circumstances the defendant's act was out of all proportion and not self-defence. Neither had the claimant consented to such a savage injury by taking part in a fight.

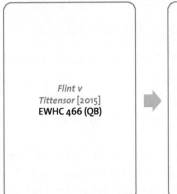

*Flint v Tittensor* [2015] **EWHC 466 (QB)**

F became separated from his friends on a night out and his mobile phone had stopped working. He asked T, who was sitting in a car, if he could use his phone. T refused in an aggressive manner and F banged on the bonnet of the car causing a dent. T then drove at F knocking him on to the bonnet before shaking him off. F fell to the ground and suffered head injuries.

The court considered a number of issues including whether T was liable in trespass and whether he could claim self-defence. It was held that driving at F was the application of force and a battery. T was not in any physical danger from F and using his car to drive at him when he could have driven away was unreasonable. His defence of self-defence failed.

## Lawful arrest

The police have certain powers of arrest both at common law and under statute. If they use these powers according to the rules they may lawfully commit assault, battery and false imprisonment. The main statute is the **Police and Criminal Evidence Act 1984** as amended.

## Contributory negligence

The defence of contributory negligence is not available for intentional torts like trespass to the person and the Law Reform (Contributory Negligence) Act 1945 does not apply. This was confirmed in *Co-operative Group Ltd v Pritchard* [2011] EWCA Civ 329.

# The tort of *Wilkinson v Downton*

The torts of assault, battery and false imprisonment are all caused by intentional acts which directly harm the claimant. The tort of *Wilkinson v Downton* is the intentional infliction of physical harm. But this harm is caused indirectly rather than directly so the defendant does not actually touch the claimant.

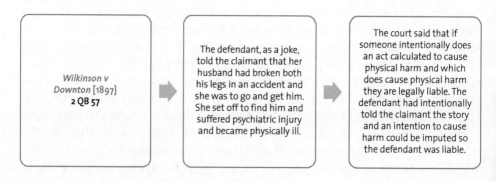

*Wilkinson v Downton* [1897] 2 QB 57

The defendant, as a joke, told the claimant that her husband had broken both his legs in an accident and she was to go and get him. She set off to find him and suffered psychiatric injury and became physically ill.

The court said that if someone intentionally does an act calculated to cause physical harm and which does cause physical harm they are legally liable. The defendant had intentionally told the claimant the story and an intention to cause harm could be imputed so the defendant was liable.

In 1897 when this tort was created no claims were allowed in negligence for psychiatric harm. Neither could the claimant sue in trespass to the person as the defendant did not threaten her or touch her.

The tort of *Wilkinson v Downton* can be distinguished from trespass to the person in two ways:

❖ first, it indirectly causes harm to the claimant, and
❖ second, it requires the claimant to prove that they have suffered harm.

In *O (A Child) v Rhodes and another* [2015] UKSC 32 a claim was brought on the basis of *Wilkinson v Downton*. A father wished to publish a book about his life which contained an account of him being sexually abused when he was at school. The mother argued that if the book was published it would cause psychiatric harm to their 11 year old son who was vulnerable because he suffered from various conditions including attention deficit hyperactivity disorder. The Supreme Court said that the tort had three elements, a conduct element, a mental element and a consequences element. The consequences element required words or conduct directed at the claimant for which there was no justification. The Court of Appeal had said the book was directed at the son, there was no justification if it was likely to cause psychiatric harm to the son and that intention could be imputed to the father because he knew the son would suffer harm if he read the book. But the Supreme Court said that the father had a right to tell of his suffering and had a wide interest in telling his story to the world at large. It also said that imputing an intention had no role in the modern law of tort. There was no evidence the father had the intention to cause harm to the son. The third element of consequences needed physical or psychiatric harm and did not arise in this case. The Supreme Court reversed the decision of the Court of Appeal and said that there was no liability.

The claimant must be able to prove that they have suffered physical or psychiatric harm and they cannot claim for mere distress.

A claim under *Wilkinson v Downton* only requires one single act of harassment and this distinguishes it from a claim under the **Protection from Harassment Act 1997**.

## Harassment

The **Protection from Harassment Act 1997** created various criminal offences dealing with harassment. Under s1 harassment involves a 'course of conduct' which amounts to harassment of another and which he knows, or ought to know, amounts to harassment. Harassment includes causing alarm or distress. A course of conduct is defined in s7(3) to mean conduct on at least two occasions. This is an important difference from *Wilkinson v Downton* when only one act is required.

If harassment is proved the claimant has a right under s3 to sue in tort for damages and/or an injunction.

| *Ferguson v British Gas Ltd* [2009] EWCA Civ 46 | The claimant had been a customer of the defendant but changed to a new supplier. She continued to receive bills and letters threatening to cut off her gas supply even after she had complained about this. | The Court of Appeal said that such conduct was grave enough to amount to harassment. The defendant's argument that the letters had been generated by a computer carried no weight as they had been read by a real person. |

## Putting it into practice

Read the scenario below and answer the question.

Tom and Uri are coal miners and their union decided to take strike action. One morning they were standing in the road leading to the mine with a group of other strikers. Tom was holding a placard which read, 'We Demand a Pay Rise Now'. Val, the managing director of the mine, was driving into work in her limousine and slowed down as she approached the striking miners. Tom banged his placard on the roof of her car and shouted, 'I'm going to punch you tomorrow'. Val just drove on laughing.

Wilf, a working miner, drove towards the group of striking miners. Uri stood in his way shouting abuse and banging on the bonnet of his car. Wilf stopped his car and wound down the window and shouted back. He then reversed his car and drove at Uri knocking him to the ground and injuring him.

Yosek, another working miner, went down the mine for his shift. After working for an hour he decided to join the strikers and asked to be taken to the surface but the lift operator refused to do so until the end of the shift.

**Advise Val, Uri, Wilf and Yosek of any claims they may make in tort.**

## Outline answer – trespass to the person, assault, battery and false imprisonment

❖  *Val v Tom*

   ❖  Trespass to the person; assault: an act causing someone to fear an immediate battery; the courts apply an objective test; was the claimant put in fear of being hit?

   ❖  It has to be an immediate battery, in *Thomas v NUM*, the miners on the coach were safe. Val does not have to be afraid but simply believe she will be hit; if her car has not stopped she is probably unlikely to be hit and probably not in fear of battery.

   ❖  Consider the effect of words; in *Tuberville v Savage* the defendant's words qualified his act of putting his hand on his sword and meant it was not an assault; here Tom's words mean he is not going to do anything immediately.

   ❖  Val's claim will fail.

❖  *Uri v Wilf*

   ❖  Wilf driving at Uri is a battery, the application of unlawful force to another person; there does not have to be personal contact.

   ❖  There is intention to apply force and the intention is also hostile, *Wilson v Pringle*.

   ❖  Can Wilf claim self-defence? Is he in fear of being hit by Uri banging on his car? Wilf must only use reasonable force; this is not reasonable force to drive at Uri, *Flint v Tittensor*.

❖   *Wilf v Uri*

  ❖   Uri banging on the car; assault; is Wilf put in fear of an immediate battery? If so it is an assault; Wilf is in the car but the window is open, if in fear an assault; can argue either way.

❖   *Yosek v mine owners*

  ❖   False imprisonment: there must be a restraint and it must be total; there is a restraint here and there is no reasonable way out, *Bird v Jones*.
  ❖   It seems to be false imprisonment, but his contract is to work shifts; apply *Herd v Weardale Steel Co* where the miners voluntarily went down the mine; not false imprisonment.

# Table of key cases referred to in this chapter

| Key case | Area of law | Principle |
|---|---|---|
| *Bird v Jones* (1845) 7 QB 742 | The claimant was stopped from walking through an enclosure on a bridge but could have gone back and crossed the bridge on the other side. He had not been falsely imprisoned. | For false imprisonment there must be a total restraint and no reasonable way out. |
| *Re F* [1990] 2 AC 1 | An incompetent adult woman was sterilised without her consent. | In the House of Lords Lord Goff said that he doubted that an act had to be hostile to be a battery. |
| *Lane v Holloway* [1968] 1 QB 379 | The 23 year old defendant punched the drunk, 64 year old claimant once in the face causing serious injury. The defence of self-defence failed. | A person can only claim self-defence if in all the circumstances the force used is reasonable. |
| *Meering v Grahame-White Aviation Co Ltd* (1919) 122 LT 44 | Unknown to the claimant two works policemen stood outside the room and would have stopped him leaving. This was false imprisonment. | There is no need to know that you are falsely imprisoned. |
| *Robinson v Balmain New Ferry Co* [1910] AC 295 | The claimant paid one penny to go on a ferry and went into an enclosure. He changed his mind but refused to pay another penny to leave. It was held it was not false imprisonment. | A reasonable condition which the claimant has agreed to will not make it false imprisonment. |

| Key case | Area of law | Principle |
|---|---|---|
| *Stephens v Myers* (1830) 4 C&P 349 | At a meeting the defendant clenched his fist and walked towards the claimant but was stopped before reaching him. This was an assault. | If a person puts another in fear of being hit immediately that is an assault. |
| *Thomas v National Union of Mineworkers* [1985] 2 All ER 1 | Striking miners shouted abuse and made threats to working miners on a bus which was behind a police cordon. The miners on the bus were safe. This was not an assault. | For an assault the claimant must believe that they are in immediate danger of being hit. |
| *Wilkinson v Downton* [1897] 2 QB 57 | The defendant told the claimant that her husband had broken his legs in an accident, as a joke. She suffered psychiatric harm. The defendant was liable. | If someone by an intentional but indirect act causes another to suffer physical or psychiatric harm they are liable under *Wilkinson v Downton*. |
| *Wilson v Pringle* [1968] 2 All ER 440 | One schoolboy pulled another's school bag off his shoulder causing him to fall and break his hip. The Court of Appeal said this was not a hostile act and not a battery. | The court said that an act had to be hostile to be a battery. But see *Re F* [1990] in the House of Lords above. |

@ Visit the book's companion website to test your knowledge

❖ Resources include a subject map, revision tip podcasts, downloadable diagrams, MCQ quizzes for each chapter and a flashcard glossary

❖ www.routledge.com/cw/optimizelawrevision

# 7

# Occupiers' Liability

## Revision objectives

**Understand the law**
- Can you explain who is an 'occupier' and who is a 'visitor' under the Occupier's Liability Act (OLA) 1957?
- Can you identify the three special categories of visitor under the OLA 1957?
- Can you list the possible defences to a claim under the OLA 1957?
- Can you identify the three requirements to establish a duty under s1(3) OLA 1984?
- Can you explain three defences under the OLA 1984?

**Remember the details**
- Can you explain the common duty of care under the OLA 1957?
- Can you explain the duty to child visitors under the OLA 1957 and at common law?
- Can you distinguish between a warning and exclusion notice under the OLA 1957?
- Can you explain the three requirements under s1(3) OLA 1984 and give examples to illustrate?
- Can you explain why the defendant was not liable in *Tomlinson v Congleton BC*?

**Reflect critically on areas of debate**
- Can you explain the distinction between liability for defects with the land and for activities on the land and whether this is significant?
- Can you explain two cases on obvious risks and why no duty was owed?
- Can you explain how the age of a child may help to determine who is liable for their injuries?

**Contextualise**
- Do you understand that a claim may often equally be made for negligence or under the OLA 1957?
- Do you understand it may sometimes be difficult to determine which OLA applies?
- Do you appreciate the need to consider the defences available to a claim under the OLAs?

**Apply your skills and knowledge**
- Can you answer the question at the end of the chapter?

# Chapter Map

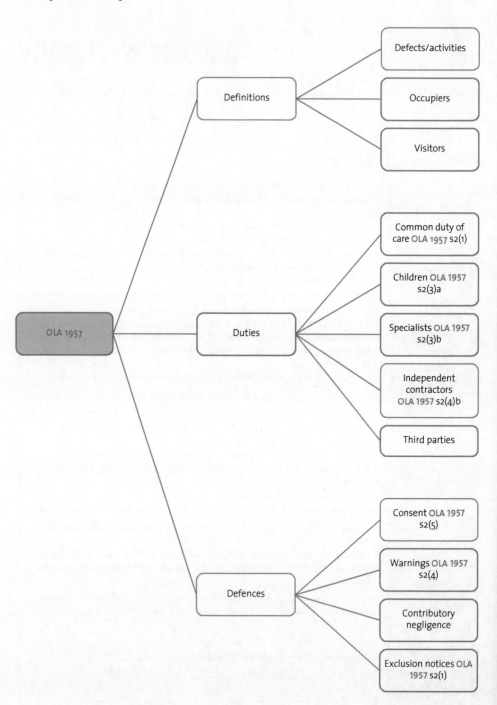

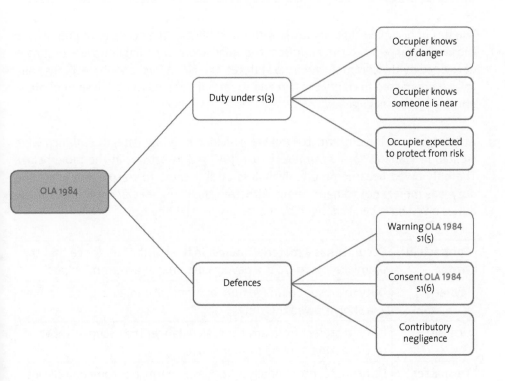

# Introduction

The tort of occupiers' liability deals with the liability of the occupier of premises to those who come on to the premises. The rules about such liability were originally developed by the common law. Two statutes, the Occupiers' Liability Acts 1957 and 1984, were passed to clarify the law and to set out detailed rules. These rules are in effect statutory negligence.

At common law the entrants to land were divided into four categories which were created in *Addie & Sons v Dumbreck* [1929] AC 358 as set out in the table below. The duty owed became progressively less until it came to trespassers when the duty was merely not to harm them. Although the categories are still relevant the duties owed have been changed by the Occupiers' Liability Acts.

| Contractual visitor | Occupier has a material interest in their visit. Duty to see that the premises are safe, e.g. a paying customer at a swimming pool |
|---|---|
| Invitee | Duty to prevent damage from an unusual danger, e.g. a customer in a shop is owed this duty |
| Licensee | Duty to protect from any concealed danger the occupier knows of, e.g. asking a friend to your house |
| Trespasser | Duty not to intentionally or recklessly harm, e.g. someone climbs over your garden wall |

The common law rules are still relevant as s1 Occupiers' Liability Act 1957 (OLA 1957) provides that visitors are those who were invitees or licensees at common law. The OLA 1957 also includes contractual visitors under s5(1). All these three categories are now 'visitors' and owed the common duty of care under s2(1) OLA 1957. Trespassers are now covered by the OLA 1984.

If an entrant to land falls outside the rules of both Occupiers' Liability Acts then the common law rules apply to them. In *British Railways Board v Herrington* [1972] AC 877 the House of Lords said that trespassers were owed a 'duty of common humanity' which is the minimum level of protection.

# The Occupiers' Liability Act 1957

## Definitions

### Distinction between defects and activities

The old common law rules made a distinction between defects with premises which caused harm and activities on the premises which caused harm.

The OLA 1957 s1(1) provides that the Act shall apply 'due to the state of the premises or to things done ... on them'; while s1(2) refers to harm suffered 'in consequence of a person's occupation or control of premises'. This is contradictory as it first provides the Act applies to both defects and activities and then provides for liability only in respect of occupation of premises.

It is generally accepted that the Act only applies to dangers arising from the condition of the premises and not activities on the premises.

> ### Examples
>
> A hole in the floor which causes a visitor to trip and injure themselves (claim under the OLA 1957).
>
> A visitor being knocked down by a car whilst on the premises (claim in negligence).

This distinction does not really matter because whether the OLA 1957 applies or the rules of negligence, the result is likely to be the same. This can be illustrated by *Ward v Tesco* [1976] 1 All ER 219 in which the claimant slipped in some yoghurt on the floor of the defendant's shop. It was held by the Court of Appeal that this could not have happened if the floor had been kept clean and the defendant was liable in negligence. The claim could equally have been under the OLA 1957.

### What the duty covers

Under the OLA 1957 there is liability for personal injury, death and damage to property.

### Premises

The OLA 1957 does not define premises but under s1(3)(a) it covers 'the obligations of a person occupying or having control over any fixed or movable structure including any vessel, vehicle or aircraft'. The OLA 1957 has been held to apply to a ladder, *Wheeler v Coppas* [1981] 3 All ER 405.

### Occupier

The OLA 1957 does not define occupier but provides that the common law rules apply. The House of Lords established that there may be more than one occupier in the next case.

| | | |
|---|---|---|
| *Wheat v Lacon & Co* [1966] **AC 522** | Mr R was the manager of the defendant's pub. The claimant's husband was a lodger in the pub and when going downstairs in the dark, in the private part of the pub he fell and was killed. Someone had stolen the light bulb on the staircase. | The court said that an occupier is someone who has some degree of control over the premises. Both Mr R and the defendants were held to be 'occupiers' as both had some degree of control over the premises and owed the common duty of care. But they were not in breach of that duty because of the act of a stranger. |

The important factor is the legal right of control rather than physical possession of the premises. In *Harris v Birkenhead Corporation* [1976] 1 All ER 341 the defendant put a compulsory purchase order on a house. The occupants moved out without telling the defendant. The defendant did not take possession of the house. A four year old child went into the house, fell out of the window and was injured. It was held that the defendant was the occupier because they had the right of control.

## Who is a visitor?

A visitor is anyone with express or implied permission to be on the premises.

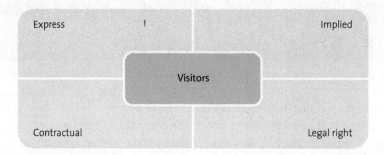

| Visitors under OLA 1957 | Non-visitors |
|---|---|
| ❖ Express visitor, e.g. asking a milkman to deliver milk.<br>❖ Implied visitor, e.g. the postman delivering letters.<br>❖ Contractual visitor: OLA 1957 s5(1) provides that if there is no contractual term dealing with the duty owed there is an implied term that such a visitor is owed the common duty of care, e.g. someone visiting the swimming baths or the cinema.<br>❖ Legal right to enter premises, e.g. a fire officer putting out a fire, a police officer with a search warrant s2(6). | ❖ Public right of way: someone using a public footpath is not a visitor under the OLA 1957 nor are they covered by the OLA 1984. They are only owed a common law duty.<br>❖ Private right of way: you give your neighbour a right of way through your garden; a duty is owed under the OLA 1984. |

Even if someone has permission to enter premises, this permission may be limited by time, area or purpose.

- ❖ Time: if you stay in a shop after closing you become a trespasser.
- ❖ Area: if a hotel guest goes through a door marked 'Private' they become a trespasser.
- ❖ Purpose: if you go into a shop to steal you are a trespasser.

What if a hotel guest is lost and looking for a toilet? In *Pearson v Coleman Brothers* [1948] 2 KB 359 the claimant, aged seven, visited a circus. She wished to go to the toilet but none were provided and in looking for a suitable place she wandered into the animal enclosure. She was attacked by a lion which put its claws through the bars of a cage. It was held that as the area was not marked off she was not a trespasser and the defendants were liable.

## The common duty of care

Under the OLA 1957 s2(1) an occupier owes the common duty of care to all his visitors. Under s2(2) this is a duty to take such care as in all the circumstances is reasonable to see that the visitor is reasonably safe in using the premises for the purposes he is invited.

- ❖ It is the visitor that must be safe not the premises.
- ❖ The common duty of care under the OLA 1957 is the same as the duty of care in negligence.
- ❖ In determining the common duty of care the courts take into account the same factors as a claim in negligence, for example, risk of harm, seriousness of the possible injury and the cost of avoiding the harm.
- ❖ Under s2(1) the occupier can extend, restrict, modify or exclude his duty.

An occupier does not need to warn of obvious dangers.

| *Darby v National Trust* [2001] EWCA Civ 189 | ➡ | The defendant owned land including a lake which was open to the public. The claimant's husband went swimming in the lake and drowned. The claimant argued that the defendant was in breach of its duty under s2(1) OLA 1957 for not providing a warning of the danger. | ➡ | It was held by the Court of Appeal that warning against swimming in the lake would not have told the claimant's husband anything he did not know already. The court said that it was like swimming in the sea and there was no need to warn of the dangers. No duty to warn and the defendant was not liable. |

## Aim Higher

Read *Tomlinson v Congleton Borough Council & Another* [2003] 3 WLR 705 especially the speeches of Lord Hoffmann and Lord Hobhouse.

They explain the scope of the common duty of care and the balance the courts are trying to strike between fulfilling that duty and allowing people the freedom to take risks.

## Special categories of visitors

| Children | Specialists | Independent contractors |
|---|---|---|
| Higher duty owed because they take less care than adults | Duty owed to specialists but not for the normal risks of their job | Occupier not liable for acts of contractor if three checks are satisfactorily completed |

### Children

'An occupier must be prepared for children to be less careful than adults' s2(3)(a).

The courts expect occupiers to take more care when dealing with children. Children have less experience of life than adults and the courts developed the doctrine of allurements. If there was something on the land which was attractive to children then they could be treated as implied visitors and owed a duty rather than classed as trespassers. In *Glasgow Corporation v Taylor* [1922] 1 AC 44 a seven year old boy picked some poisonous red berries from a bush in a public park, ate them and died. It was held that the berries were an allurement and the child could be regarded as an implied visitor instead of a trespasser. No warning had been given and the Corporation was liable.

## Common Pitfall

The doctrine of allurements was developed by the courts to provide protection for child trespassers. The **OLA 1984** now provides a duty is owed to trespassers if certain conditions are met and the doctrine is no longer needed.

However, the fact something is an allurement may be one factor taken into account by the courts in determining liability.

### Case precedent – *Jolley v Sutton LBC* [2000] 3 All ER 409

**Facts:** An old boat was abandoned on the claimant's housing estate. The claimant, aged 14, propped up the boat to try and fix it but he was injured when it fell on him. The Court of Appeal held that it was not reasonably foreseeable that someone would jack up the boat and the council were not liable.

**Principle:** The House of Lords said that it was foreseeable that children would meddle with the boat and copy adult behaviour by fixing it. The council were liable under the OLA 1957.

**Application:** The House of Lords said that the ingenuity of children should never be under estimated, which means their inventiveness. This is an important fact which courts must be aware of when dealing with claims by children under the OLA 1957.

It is often difficult to determine whether a particular act is foreseeable and this was illustrated in *Cockbill v Riley* [2013] EWHC 656. The claimant, aged 16, had just finished his GCSEs. To celebrate he went to a party with school friends including the defendant's daughter, at the defendant's house. Someone brought a paddling pool and the defendant filled it with water. After some alcoholic drinks the claimant did a belly flop into the pool and broke his back. It was held that it was foreseeable that someone might suffer a minor injury but not that someone would dive or belly flop into the pool. The defendant was not liable.

❖ If children are very young the occupier can expect the parents to have the primary responsibility for them. This does not take away the occupiers' responsibility completely. The courts will take into account the nature of the danger and the age of the child.

*Phipps v Rochester Corporation* [1955] 1 QB 450 ➡ The claimant, aged five, and his sister, aged seven, went blackberry picking on a building site. The defendants, who owned the site, knew that children played there. The boy fell in a trench and broke his leg. The danger was obvious to an adult but not to a child. ➡ The court said that an occupier can assume that little children will be accompanied by a responsible person. The defendant was not liable.

This principle was followed in *Bourne Leisure v Marsden* [2009] EWCA Civ 671 in which a two year old boy wandered off from his mother at a holiday park and drowned in a pond. At first instance it was held that the defendant was in breach of the common duty of care for not giving warnings. The Court of Appeal said that the source of danger was obvious. There was no duty to fence all the ponds in the holiday park and the defendant could expect parents to supervise small children. The defendant was not liable. The court also stressed that the parents were not to blame either and that a child can sometimes wander off without any fault on the part of the parents.

## Common Pitfall

The **OLA 1957** s2(3)(a) sets out the duty of the occupier to children. But the duty to young children was developed by the common law in *Phipps v Rochester Corporation* [1955] that very young children should be supervised by an adult.

### Specialists

An occupier may expect that a skilled person working on the premises will guard against the ordinary risks of their job (OLA 1957 s2(3)(b)).

## Example

If a roofer slips and falls off a roof they have been asked to fix the occupier will not be liable.

The occupier does owe the common duty of care to specialists but not in respect of the normal risks of their job. In *Roles v Nathan* [1963] 2 All ER 908 the claimant brothers were chimney sweeps engaged to clean the flue on an old boiler. The defendant's engineer told them not to work with a fire lit because of the danger of carbon monoxide fumes. They did work with the fire lit and were killed by the fumes. It was held by the Court of Appeal that they knew the danger and it was up to them to guard against it. The occupier was not liable.

If a specialist is injured from a risk of the job an occupier may be liable if the specialist acted with skill. In *Ogwo v Taylor* [1988] AC 431 a fire officer was injured fighting a house fire which was started negligently and the occupier was liable.

### Independent contractors

Section 2(4)(b) OLA 1957 provides that the occupier is not liable for damage caused to a visitor due to the faulty execution of 'work of construction, maintenance or repair' by an independent contractor if the occupier acted reasonably:

❖ In giving the work to the contractor. It is reasonable to give skilled or technical work to an expert and it may be reasonable to give basic work to a contractor, for example, cleaning.

❖ By taking reasonable steps to check that the contractor was competent. This may involve checking that the contractor is a member of a trade association and checking that they have insurance.
❖ By checking that the work was completed properly. It would not be reasonable to expect the occupier to check technical work but the occupier could check a simple matter such as steps being cleared of ice (*Woodward v Mayor of Hastings* [1945] KB 74).

In *Haseldine v Daw Ltd* [1941] 2 KB 343 the defendant owned a block of flats and engaged a reputable firm of engineers to service the lift. The following day the claimant was injured when the lift fell to the bottom of the lift shaft. It was held that the defendant was not liable as it was reasonable to employ a specialist and the defendant could not check the work.

## Third parties
An occupier may be liable for the actions of third parties which cause harm to visitors on the premises if the occupier has control over those third parties. In *Cunningham v Reading FC Ltd* (1991) 157 LG Rev 481 a football match took place between Reading FC and Bristol City FC at the defendant's ground. Some Bristol City FC fans rioted, broke off pieces of concrete from the terraces and threw them at the claimant police officers who were on duty. The claimants argued that there had been trouble before between the fans and the defendants were in breach of their duty under the OLA 1957. It was held that although the damage was caused by Bristol City FC fans the defendants knew from previous incidents that concrete could be broken off. The defendants were liable under the OLA 1957.

## Defences

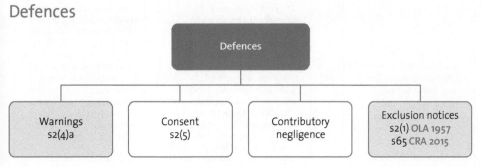

## Warnings
Section 2(4)(a) provides that if damage is caused by something the visitor has been warned about, that is not enough to avoid liability by the occupier unless the warning was enough to enable the visitor to be reasonably safe.

In *Roles v Nathan* [1963] Lord Denning gave the following example to illustrate how s2(4) would work.

- If the only way into premises was by a rotten footbridge over a stream and the occupier put up a notice, 'This bridge is dangerous', then under s2(4) if the visitor was injured using the bridge the occupier would be liable.
- If there were two footbridges, a rotten one and a safe one and the occupier put up a notice, 'Do not use this footbridge. It is dangerous. There is a safe one further up-stream.' This warning enables the visitor to be safe. If the visitor used the rotten bridge and was injured the occupier would not be liable.

The courts in deciding if the warning is sufficient to enable the visitor to be safe take a range of factors into account including:

- Is the warning sign large enough?
- Is the sign in a prominent place?
- Does it specify the danger? (*Rae v Mars Ltd* [1990] 3 EG 80)
- How old is the visitor?
- Can the visitor read?
- Is the warning enough or is the danger so great that a barrier is required?
- Is the danger obvious? (*Darby v National Trust* [2001])

In *Rae v Mars Ltd* [1990] a surveyor entered an unlit storeroom, fell down a one metre drop from the doorway and broke his ankle. It was held that because of the exceptional nature of this danger he should have been given a specific warning about it. This was a breach of the common duty of care under s2(1) OLA 1957. However, because he did not switch on his torch the claimant's damages were reduced by one-third for contributory negligence. In *Taylor v English Heritage* [2016] it was argued that the defendant was in breach of s2 OLA 1957 for failing to warn.

| *Taylor v English Heritage* [2016] EWCA Civ 448 | The defendants were the occupiers of a castle which was open to the public. There was a platform with two cannons on it. A steep slope below the platform led to a grass path with a four metre drop from one side of the path into a dry moat. The claimant went down the steep slope but slipped, fell in the moat and suffered a severe head injury.  | The county court said that the defendant was in breach of duty under s2 OLA 1957 for failing to warn of the danger. The Court of Appeal held that the drop was not an obvious danger to someone on the platform. The risk of going down a steep slope was very different to one with a four metre drop. The defendant was liable. |
| --- | --- | --- |

## Consent

Under s2(5) the occupier is not liable for risks which the visitor willingly accepts. In *Simms v Leigh RFC* [1969] 2 All ER 923 the claimant, a rugby league player, was thrown against a concrete wall during a game and injured. The wall was two metres from the touch line and it met league standards. It was held that the claimant had accepted the risks of playing at his home stadium and the defendant was not liable.

## Contributory negligence

The OLA 1957 does not mention contributory negligence but the courts have reduced damages if the visitor is partly to blame. In *Taylor v English Heritage* [2016] the claimant was found to be 50% contributorily negligent.

## Exclusion notices

Under the OLA 1957 s2(1) an occupier may extend, restrict, modify or exclude his duty to any visitor by agreement or otherwise. However, under the Consumer Rights Act 2015 s65(1) a trader cannot by the term of a consumer contract or notice exclude or restrict liability for death or personal injury resulting from negligence. Under s65(2) a person is not to be taken as having accepted any risk merely because they agreed to or knew about the term or notice. The right given to an occupier under s2(1) of OLA 1957 to exclude liability is restricted in the case of businesses as regards injury or death. Any such notice will be void.

### Common Pitfall

It is important to realise the distinction between a warning and an exclusion notice. A warning notice is subject to s2(4)(a) OLA 1957 and it must be sufficient to enable the visitor to be reasonably safe. It may need to be in a prominent place, to tell the visitor what the danger is and even how to avoid the danger.

An exclusion notice is the occupier trying to exclude themselves from liability. These are subject to s65(2) of the Consumer Rights Act 2015 and cannot exclude liability for death or injury arising from negligence in the course of a business.

# The Occupiers' Liability Act 1984

## Introduction

The original common law rule on trespassers was that no duty was owed to trespassers as long as the occupier did not intentionally harm them. The OLA 1957 does not apply to trespassers. Before the OLA 1984 was passed the courts gave trespassers some protection by developing the concept of the 'implied visitor', for example, *Glasgow Corporation v Taylor* [1922]. In *British Railways Board v Herrington* [1972] a six year old boy climbed through a hole in a fence on to an electrified railway line and was burned. The hole was near a station and the stationmaster knew that it was used as a short cut. The House of Lords held that the defendant owed a duty of 'common humanity' to the claimant trespasser and was liable.

## Who does the OLA 1984 apply to?

Under s1(1)(a) the OLA 1984 applies to 'persons other than visitors'. This includes:

❖ trespassers;

- ❖ people using private rights of way;
- ❖ people with rights under the Countryside and Rights of Way Act 2000.

The OLA 1984 does not apply to someone using a public right of way and only the common law rules apply in that case.

## What does the duty cover?
- ❖ A duty is owed for injury due to the state of the premises or things done or omitted to be done on them (s1(1)).
- ❖ But there is no liability for loss or damage to property (s1(8)).

## Who is an occupier?
Under s1(2)(a) occupier has the same meaning as under the OLA 1957 and is someone with a sufficient degree of control over the land. A mere right of access is not sufficient to give control, *Bailey v Armes* [1999] EGCS 21.

## When is a duty owed under the Act?

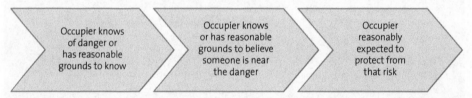

Under s1(3) a duty is owed if the occupier:

(a) is aware of the danger or has reasonable grounds to know about it; and
(b) knows or has reasonable grounds to believe that someone is near the danger or may come near it; and
(c) the risk is one which in all the circumstances the occupier may reasonably be expected to provide some protection.

All three requirements must be met for a duty to be owed. They were applied in the following cases.

### Case precedent – *Ratcliff v McConnell* [1998] 1 WLR 670

**Facts:** The defendants owned a college with an outdoor swimming pool. At the end of each day the pool was locked. A notice on the gate stated that the pool must not be used between 10.00 pm and 6.30 am. The claimant was a 19 year old student at the college. Early one winter morning he climbed over the gates and dived into the pool. The water was shallow and he hit his head on the bottom of the pool and was paralysed. Although the claimant was a student when he climbed over the gate he became a trespasser.

**Principle:** The Court of Appeal said the defendants knew of the danger, the pool. Even if they knew students climbed over the gates to swim they did not have to warn them of the danger. Diving into a pool at night was an obvious danger to an adult.

**Application:** The courts have consistently applied this principle that if the danger is obvious to an adult there is no need to warn them about it. It would be different for a child.

In *Tomlinson v Congleton Borough Council & Another* [2003] the defendants owned a country park with a lake which was open to the public. A notice by the lake stated, 'Dangerous water: no swimming'. The claimant, aged 18, was standing in the lake with the water below his knees. He then dived into the lake, struck his head on the bottom and was paralysed. The defendants knew that people ignored the signs. The claimant was a lawful visitor to the park but became a trespasser when he entered the lake.

The Court of Appeal said that the lake was an attraction, the notices were ineffective and not enough had been done to fulfil the duty so the defendant was liable.

In the House of Lords it was held that the risk was not from the state of the premises but from the claimant's own act, diving into shallow water. The defendants were not liable. Lord Hoffmann applied s1(3) of the OLA 1984: (a) the occupier was aware of the danger to anyone diving into the lake; (b) the occupier knew that people were near the lake; and (c) was the risk one that the occupier should have offered protection from? The answer was no, because the danger of diving into shallow water was obvious. The defendants did not owe a duty under s1(3).

| | | |
|---|---|---|
| *Keown v Coventry Healthcare NHS Trust* [2006] **EWCA Civ 39** | The claimant, an 11 year old boy, frequently played in the grounds of the defendant's hospital with his friends. The defendants knew that the public used the grounds as a short cut. The claimant climbed on to the underside of a fire escape from the ground, fell about 9 metres and suffered brain injuries. At first instance it was held that the defendants were liable because they knew that children played in the grounds. | The Court of Appeal said that the claimant knew the risks and had admitted that he should not have been climbing on the fire escape. The risk of injury was not due to the state of the premises and the defendants were not liable. |

In determining whether the occupier has acted reasonably under s1(3)(c) the courts take a number of factors into account including:

- the nature of the risk;
- whether the entry was accidental or intentional;
- the age of the trespasser;
- the cost of precautions.

## Defences

| Warnings | Consent | Exclusions |
|---|---|---|
| Section 1(5) 'Any duty owed … may … be discharged by taking such steps as are reasonable in all the circumstances of the case to give warning of the danger.' The duty is on the occupier. The warning must take into account the nature of the danger, the age of the trespasser etc. In the case of children consider if a warning is enough to discharge the duty. | Section 1(6) 'No duty is owed … to any person in respect of risks willingly accepted.' In *Ratcliff v McConnell* [1998] the 19 year old claimant accepted the risks by climbing over a locked gate and diving into the pool. | There is no provision under the OLA 1984 for the occupier to exclude liability. |

### Contributory negligence

The OLA 1984 does not mention contributory negligence but the courts have applied the rules from the Law Reform (Contributory Negligence) Act 1945 to claims under the OLA 1984.

# Putting it into practice

Read the question below and attempt an outline answer.

Lord Ashok owns a fifteenth century castle and a lake in grounds of 400 acres which is surrounded by a high wall. Due to the recession he decides to open the castle to the public and charge an entrance fee. One of the highlights of a visit is the Knights' Room which contains suits of armour. Recently, Lord Ashok had found Faria on the internet, a specialist in medieval armour and engaged her to polish the suits of armour.

Carla and her partner Dipan visit the castle with their four year old daughter, Eli, and pay at the entrance. The first place they go to is the Knights' Room. When they are looking round Dipan leaves the room to find a toilet. While Carla is chatting to another mother Eli touches one of the suits of armour which topples over and cuts her arm. Faria had forgotten to re-attach it to its metal bolt in the wall which would have kept it secure.

Meanwhile on the way back from the toilet Dipan sees a notice across an entrance which states, 'Danger – Keep Away'. He goes through the entrance into a great hall which is part of the castle being repaired by George, a builder. An old beam falls from the roof and hits Dipan causing head injuries.

Holly, aged 14, who lives in the local village often climbs over the wall to go swimming in the lake with her friends. A big sign by the lake states, 'No Swimming'. They had been chased away by the castle security guards on several occasions. One afternoon Holly climbs over the wall, goes swimming in the lake and gashes her leg on an old bike on the bottom of the lake.

**Advise Eli, Dipan and Holly of the claims they may make, if any, under the** Occupiers' Liability Acts.

## Outline answer – Occupiers' Liability Acts 1957 and 1984

❖ *Eli v Lord Ashok and Faria*

   ❖ Eli is a lawful visitor to the castle as Carla has paid for her and she is owed the common duty of care under the OLA 1957 s2(1).

   ❖ Under s2(3) occupiers must be prepared for children to be less careful than adults, *Glasgow Corporation v Taylor* which imposes a higher duty. With very young children it is expected that parents will be responsible, *Phipps v Rochester Corporation* where the occupier was not liable for a five year old injured on a building site. Application: this seems a dangerous place for a four year old, should her parents be looking after her?

   ❖ Faria: under s2(4)b OLA 1957 the occupier is not liable for damage caused by an independent contractor if three conditions are met. It is reasonable to engage Faria to do the work; but has Lord Ashok checked she was competent? He simply found her on the internet. Has he checked the work? In *Woodward v Mayor of Hastings* the occupier was liable for not checking the ice had been cleared from the step. It would be simple to check the work and could be argued that Lord Ashok is liable rather than Faria.

   ❖ If it is argued Eli should not have been left, her parents are liable.

❖ *Dipan v Lord Ashok and George*

   ❖ Dipan is a lawful visitor to the castle and is owed the common duty of care under the OLA 1957 s2(1). Here there are two occupiers Lord Ashok and George, *Wheat v Lacon* as both have some control over the great hall.

❖ When Dipan goes into the great hall he becomes a trespasser. The OLA 1984 s1(3) applies; does the occupier know of the danger, the state of the castle? The answer would be yes. Does the occupier know there are people near the danger? There is a notice stating keep away but there are visitors in the castle; is the occupier reasonably expected to protect from this risk? Could be seriously injured and should be protected.

❖ Under s1(5) is the warning reasonable? In *Ratcliff v McConnell* there was no need to warn as the danger was obvious; could the fact this is a building site be seen from the entrance or not? If it could, Dipan should not have gone in; but even if it could not be seen Dipan is an adult and the warning may be sufficient to avoid liability. Consider if an obvious danger.

❖ *Holly v Lord Ashok*

   ❖ Holly is a trespasser; she is injured due to the state of the premises.

   ❖ She may be owed a duty if the three requirements under the OLA 1984 s1(3) are met. Does the occupier know of the danger? Which is the state of the lake, presumably he does or should know; does he know people are near it; children have been chased away so this condition could be met; is it something the occupier is expected to protect people from? This point is arguable either way although it could cause serious harm.

   ❖ Consider the effect of the sign: under s1(5) it must be reasonable; but it fails to state what the danger is; Holly is a child and the occupier may still owe her a duty.

   ❖ Has Holly consented under s1(6) as she has been swimming on several occasions? In *Keown v Coventry Healthcare NHS Trust* [2006] EWCA Civ 39 the claimant who was 11 years old admitted he was doing wrong. Could Holly's case be distinguished as the danger is hidden? If so the occupier would be liable.

# Table of key cases referred to in this chapter

| Key case | Area of law | Principle |
|---|---|---|
| *Darby v National Trust* [2001] EWCA Civ 189 | The claimant's husband went swimming in the defendant's lake and drowned. Argued that the defendant was in breach of duty under OLA 1957 s2(1) as no warning signs. | It was held that there was no need to warn about obvious dangers. This is the important principle. |
| *Haseldine v Daw* [1941] 2 KB 343 | The defendant's lift had just been serviced by an independent contractor. It fell to the bottom of the shaft and the claimant was injured. | The independent contractor is liable for harm to visitors not the occupier if the three conditions from the OLA 1957 s2(4)(b) are met. |

| | | |
|---|---|---|
| *Jolley v Sutton LBC* [2000] 3 All ER 409 | A 14 year old boy was injured when an abandoned boat he was fixing on the defendant's housing estate fell on him. It was foreseeable children would meddle with the boat and the defendant was liable under OLA 1957. | The House of Lords said that children's inventiveness should never be underestimated. |
| *Phipps v Rochester Corporation* [1955] 1 QB 450 | A five year old boy fell in a trench on the defendant's building site and was injured. The defendants were not liable. | An occupier can expect young children to be supervised by parents. |
| *Ratcliff v McConnell* [1998] 1 WLR 705 | The 19 year old claimant trespasser climbed over a locked gate and dived into a swimming pool at night. He was badly injured and claimed under s1(3) OLA 1984. No duty owed. | There was no need to warn of an obvious danger. |
| *Roles v Nathan* [1963] 2 All ER 908 | Two chimney sweeps were killed by carbon monoxide fumes from a boiler they were cleaning. The occupier was not liable. | Under s2(3)(b) OLA 1957 specialists should guard against the risks of their job. |
| *Taylor v English Heritage* [2016] EWCA Civ 448 | The claimant fell four metres into a moat while walking round a castle. The moat could not be seen from the claimant's starting position. The defendant had not warned of this danger and was liable under OLA 1957. | Under the OLA 1957 the occupier may need to warn visitors if a danger is not obvious. |
| *Tomlinson v Congleton Borough Council & Another* [2003] 3 WLR 705 | The 18 year old claimant trespassed, dived into the defendant's lake and was injured. He claimed under s1(3) OLA 1984 but no duty was owed. | There was nothing wrong with the state of the premises. If the danger is created by the claimant no duty is owed. |

| Key case | Area of law | Principle |
|----------|-------------|-----------|
| *Wheat v Lacon* [1966] AC 522 | The claimant's husband fell down the stairs in the dark in a pub and died. Both the manager and owner were occupiers. They were not liable as a stranger had stolen the light bulb. | There can be more than one occupier. The test is the right of control over the premises. |

@ **Visit the book's companion website to test your knowledge**

❖ Resources include a subject map, revision tip podcasts, downloadable diagrams, MCQ quizzes for each chapter and a flashcard glossary

❖ www.routledge.com/cw/optimizelawrevision

# Revision objectives

**Understand the law**
- Can you outline the three requirements to establish vicarious liability?
- Can you identify the three tests used to distinguish employees from independent contractors?
- Can you explain the Salmond test and how it has been altered?
- Can you explain the legal position with lending employees?

**Remember the details**
- Can you explain the economic reality test?
- Can you explain what is meant by dual vicarious liability?
- Can you explain the effect of a prohibition on employees illustrating your answer with cases?
- Can you explain the employer's vicarious liability for the criminal acts of employees using cases?

**Reflect critically on areas of debate**
- Can you explain the significance of 'akin to employment' using cases?
- Can you explain the effect of prohibiting employees from giving lifts?
- Can you explain how policy may be a factor in cases of vicarious liability?

**Contextualise**
- Do you understand how the tests for determining who is an employee are used in modern times?
- Do you understand the effect of the 'close connection' and 'akin to employment' tests on the law?
- Do you appreciate how the law of vicarious liability has changed to meet the needs of society?

**Apply your skills and knowledge**
- Can you analyse and comment on the changes in the law since *Lister v Hesley Hall*?
- Can you answer the question at the end of this chapter?

# Chapter Map

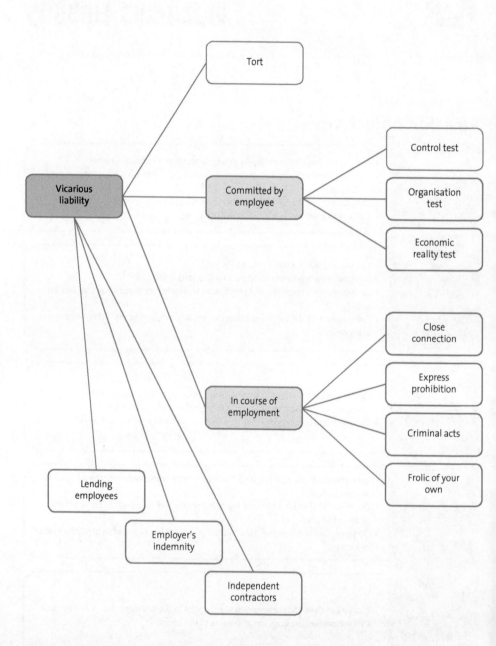

# Introduction

The rule of vicarious liability means that one person is liable for the torts of another. This is an unusual rule in tort where liability is generally based on fault, for example, someone will only be liable in negligence if they are at fault in some way.

The main example is that an employer is vicariously liable for the torts of an employee. However, the employee is primarily liable and remains liable as well as the employer. In practice an employee would only be held liable if they committed an intentional act.

A number of reasons have been advanced why the employer should be held vicariously liable:

❖ The employer can take out insurance to cover liability.
❖ It improves standards because the employer will try to ensure that the employee does not commit torts.
❖ The employer benefits from the work of the employee and should pay for losses arising from that work.
❖ The employer can pass on the loss to the consumer, for example, by increasing the price of the goods produced.

## Common Pitfall

Vicarious liability is not a tort. It is a principle that one person is liable for the torts of another.

# The requirements for vicarious liability

There are three requirements to establish vicarious liability.

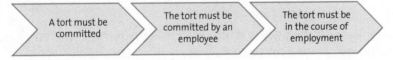

A tort must be committed → The tort must be committed by an employee → The tort must be in the course of employment

## A tort must be committed

It must be shown that the employee has committed a tort. If no tort has been committed the employer cannot be vicariously liable. Examples of torts include negligence, trespass and deceit (fraud).

## The tort must be committed by an employee

The law makes a distinction between employees and independent contractors. The employer is vicariously liable only for the torts of employees and not for the torts of independent contractors. In the latter case the independent contractor is liable for their own torts.

- ❖ An office worker or teacher will be employees.
- ❖ A plumber or barrister will be independent contractors.

The distinction is not as clear as it used to be as more people work for themselves but may spend most of their time working for one company. The courts have developed a number of tests to determine whether someone is an employee or an independent contractor.

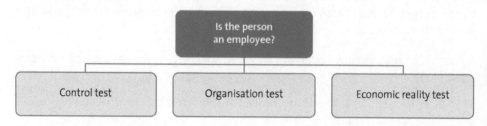

## The control test

If one person can tell another what to do and how to do it, then that other person is an employee. The test was more useful when most people were unskilled. It is of less importance in a society where the workforce are better educated and have technological skills and are unlikely to be told how to do their jobs. It is still used today but its significance is that the employer can direct what the employee does not how he does it (*Cox v Ministry of Justice* [2016] UKSC 10). It is not used as the only test to decide if someone is an employee.

## The organisation test

This test asks if a person is integrated into the organisation or is simply an accessory to the organisation. In *Cassidy v Minister of Health* [1951] 2 KB 343 the Court of Appeal held that a surgeon in a hospital was an integral part of the hospital and the hospital was vicariously liable for the surgeon's acts.

## The economic reality test

The economic reality test which is also known as the multiple test was developed in the following case and considers how a range of factors apply.

**Case precedent – *Ready Mixed Concrete v Minister of Pensions and National Insurance* [1968] 2 QB 497**

**Facts:** RMC delivered concrete. The drivers of the lorries were described as self-employed, they were paid a fixed rate per mile but were only offered work if it was available; they had to buy the lorries on hire-purchase, insure and maintain the lorries. However, the lorries had to be in company colours, drivers had to wear a uniform and had to be available when required. Were the drivers employees or independent contractors?

**Principle:** Applying the economic reality test it was held that ownership of the lorries and taking the risk of loss pointed to drivers being independent contractors.

**Application:** The factors set out below are used in addition to other relevant factors in deciding if someone is an employee.

In the above case the court set out three conditions to be an employee:

❖ a person agrees to provide work in return for payment;
❖ a person agrees, expressly or impliedly to be under the employer's control;
❖ the other terms are consistent with a contract of employment.

The following factors are considered:

❖ method of payment – if regular an employee;
❖ tax – if deducted before payment, an employee;
❖ tools – if provided, an employee;
❖ business risks – if taken, an independent contractor;
❖ hours – if regular, an employee.

## Common Pitfall

It is an easy mistake to pick one test and apply it. The courts often use a mix of these tests plus any other factors which are relevant in deciding if someone is an employee.

It is best to follow the same practice when answering problem questions.

## *Relationships akin to employment*

In recent years in deciding whether a person is an employee the courts have taken a wider view and included relationships which are 'akin to' employment relationships, which simply means close to. In *JGE v Trustees of Portsmouth RC Diocese* [2012] EWCA Civ 938 the claimant was abused by a Roman Catholic priest when she was in a children's home in the 1970s. A priest is not an employee in the traditional sense of the word and is not paid a salary or told what to do. The priest visited the children's home which was run by an order of nuns. The bishop of the diocese could dismiss the priest for gross misconduct. The Court of Appeal asked, as regards control is the person accountable to the employer for the way they do their work? Is the work a central part of the organisation? The court concluded that the relationship between them was akin to that of employment and the bishop was vicariously liable for the torts of the priest.

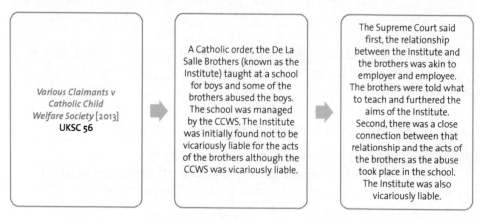

In *Cox v Ministry of Justice* [2016] the claimant was a catering manager at Swansea Prison and a number of prisoners worked in the prison kitchen. One of the prisoners was carrying a sack of rice downstairs and negligently dropped it on the claimant, injuring her. The claimant argued that the defendant was vicariously liable for the prisoner's negligence even though prisoners had no contract with the prison and were only paid a nominal wage. The Supreme Court said that in applying vicarious liability outside the relationship of employment two factors were relevant; whether the activities were integral to the business and the risk of committing the tort. Here feeding the prisoners was an integral part of the business of the prison and the defendant created the risk by giving the work to the prisoner. The defendant was therefore vicariously liable.

## Up for Debate

Please read the following article, 'Vicarious Liability: There's an App for That' by Nigel MacKay, 2016, JPILaw 2 pp 90–94.

It explains the changes in working practice to flexible ways of working.

It examines the modern two-stage test for vicarious liability: first, whether the relationship is capable of giving rise to vicarious liability; second, whether the acts were connected to that relationship in a way to give rise to vicarious liability (Lord Phillips in *Various Claimants* [2013]). It also considers the factors for determining if a relationship is akin to employment.

## Lending employees

If an employer lends an employee to a second employer and the employee commits a tort, which employer is liable?

The rules were set out in *Mersey Docks and Harbour Board v Coggins & Griffiths* [1947] AC 1. The court took into account a number of factors but the presumption was that the original employer remains liable unless it was shown that control had passed to the second employer. MDHB hired out a crane and driver to C&G. While unloading a ship the driver negligently injured someone. The agreement between MDHB and C&G provided that the driver was an employee of C&G and C&G could tell the driver what to do. MDHB still paid the driver and could dismiss him. The House of Lords held that MDHB still had the greater control over the driver and remained his employer.

The courts have said that in some circumstances instead of choosing between two employers there can be dual vicarious liability so both employers are jointly liable.

In *Viasystems v Thermal Transfer Ltd* [2005] EWCA Civ 1151 V entered a contract with TT for TT to install air conditioning in a factory. TT sub-contracted work to D Ltd who in turn sub-contracted to CAT. CAT provided two fitters, M and S, who worked under the supervision of H, who worked for D Ltd. S negligently damaged the sprinkler system with the result that the factory was flooded. V claimed that both D Ltd and CAT were vicariously liable for the action of S. The Court of Appeal said that the important factors were the right of control, who was responsible for preventing the negligent act and whether S had been integrated into both businesses. Both H and M had the right to control S and he had been integrated into both businesses, therefore there was dual vicarious liability and both D Ltd and CAT were liable.

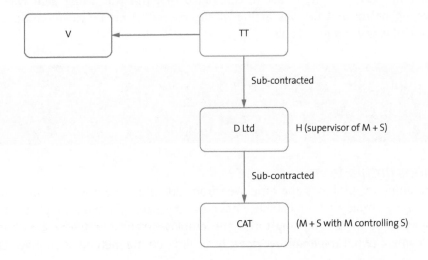

# The tort must be committed in the course of employment

## The test

The employer will only be liable if the tort was committed 'in the course of employment'. The test used to decide this is known as the Salmond test and it was first set out by Professor Salmond in a textbook in 1907.

| Is it a wrongful act which is authorised by the employer? | OR | Is it a wrongful and unauthorised way of doing an authorised act? |
|---|---|---|

The application of the second test caused some problems in the way that courts interpreted it. The House of Lords changed this test in *Lister v Hesley Hall* [2001] 2 All ER 769 (below) and substituted a new test of whether there is a 'close connection' between the employee's tort and their job.

If the employer asks the employee to commit a tort or impliedly authorises it, the employer will be vicariously liable.

## Example

The employer telling the employee to drive a lorry which the employer knows has defective brakes and the lorry crashes and injures someone.

If there is a 'close connection' between the tort and the job the employer will be vicariously liable. This can be illustrated by *Century Insurance v Northern Ireland Road Transport Board* [1942] AC 509. The defendant's tanker driver was delivering petrol to a petrol station. He lit a cigarette and threw away the match which caused an explosion. The House of Lords held that this was a negligent way of delivering petrol and he was acting in the course of his employment so the defendant was vicariously liable.

## Common Pitfall

The second part of the Salmond test is no longer used and has been replaced by the close connection test from *Lister v Hesley Hall* [2001].

## Express prohibition

If the employer prohibits the employee from doing a certain act this does not exempt the employer from liability. Otherwise the employer could simply tell the employee not to commit any torts! The employer can limit the scope of the employment (what the employee does) but a limit on the method of employment (how the employee does the job) will not be effective. Compare the decisions in the following two cases.

| Limpus v London General Omnibus Co (1862) 1 H&C 526 | Beard v London General Omnibus Co [1900] 2 QB 530 |
|---|---|
| The defendants told their bus drivers not to race rival companies. A driver was racing and caused an accident which damaged the claimant's bus. It was held that the driver was doing something he was authorised to do, driving the bus and although he was doing this in an incorrect way, he was acting within the course of his employment. | The defendant's bus conductor was employed to issue tickets on the bus. He was driving the bus and injured the claimant. It was held that driving the bus was outside the course of employment and the defendant was not vicariously liable. |

If the employer prohibits the employee from giving lifts in a company vehicle but the employee does so and negligently crashes, injuring the passenger, will the employer be vicariously liable? The cases have produced some fine distinctions.

| Twine v Beans Express (1946) 175 LT 131 | Rose v Plenty [1976] 1 WLR 141 |
|---|---|
| The defendant told their employees not to give lifts in company vehicles. An employee gave a hitchhiker a lift but crashed and the hitchhiker was killed. The Court of Appeal said that giving a lift was unauthorised and outside the course of employment. The defendant was not liable. | A milkman was told not to give anyone a lift on his milk float. He paid the 13 year old claimant to help him on his milk round. Due to the milkman's negligent driving the claimant was injured. The Court of Appeal said that the prohibited act was for the benefit of the employer and was therefore within the course of employment. |

In *Twine* (1946) the employee was still driving the company van and it could be argued he was acting in the course of employment. It seems that the distinction between these two cases is that in *Rose* [1976] obtaining the help of the boy was for the benefit of the employer. The decision is also influenced by policy in ensuring that the injured boy obtains compensation.

## Criminal acts

If an employee commits a crime the employee can be prosecuted under the criminal law. If that crime is also a tort the employer may be vicariously liable for that tort. For example, if the employee punches someone in the course of employment this is the tort of battery and the employer could be vicariously liable.

The above case shows that the act does not have to be for the benefit of the employer to be within the course of employment.

The problems with the application of the Salmond test were highlighted in *Trotman v North Yorkshire CC* [1999] IRLR 98 where a teacher sexually abused pupils on a school trip. The Court of Appeal said that this could not be an unauthorised way of doing an authorised act, which was looking after the pupils. Therefore the school were not vicariously liable.

### Case precedent – *Lister v Hesley Hall* [2001] 2 All ER 769

**Facts:** G, a warden at the defendant's boarding school for boys, sexually abused some of the boys. If the Salmond test was applied it could not be argued this was merely an unauthorised way of doing his job.

**Principle:** The House of Lords said that the test should be whether there was a 'very close connection' between the tort and the job. G's job was to look after the boys, he committed the abuse during his working hours and on the defendant's premises. There was a close connection between the tort and the job and the defendants were vicariously liable for G's torts.

**Application:** This decision was a very important step in enabling the victims of sexual abuse to obtain compensation from employers and it shows the effect of policy in changing the law. It has been applied and developed in *Cox v Ministry of Justice* [2016] and *Mohamud v Morrison Supermarkets plc* [2016] UKSC 11.

*Lister* was applied in *Mattis v Pollock* [2003] EWCA Civ 887. The defendant employed a bouncer (doorman) at his night club and encouraged him to act aggressively. One night the bouncer was involved in a fight with the claimant. The bouncer left the club, went to his flat nearby and obtained a knife. He then returned, saw the claimant in the street outside and stabbed him. The Court of Appeal said that the stabbing was not a separate incident and there was a close connection between the stabbing and the bouncer's job. The defendant was vicariously liable for the bouncer's actions.

In *Mohamud v Morrison Supermarkets plc* [2016] UKSC 11 the claimant went into the defendant's petrol station and asked if he could print some documents from a memory stick. An employee of the defendant racially abused the claimant, followed him out to the forecourt and punched and kicked him. The Court of Appeal said that the employee's duties did not involve keeping order, his actions were not to help the employer and the job did not carry a risk of the employee committing such acts. There was no close connection between the job and the act and the defendant was not vicariously liable.

The Supreme Court said that vicarious liability needed two things, a relationship between the defendant and the wrongdoer, and a connection between that relationship and the act. Here the wrongdoer was an employee so the first requirement was met. In deciding if there was a sufficient connection two matters had to be considered. First, what was the nature of the job and, second, whether there was a close connection between the job and the act. The employee's job was to serve customers, which was what he was doing and his actions could be seen as an unbroken sequence of events. The employer was vicariously liable.

This case illustrates how on such facts liability can be argued both ways and the close connection test is open to interpretation.

## Aim Higher

It is important to understand how the courts apply the tests to determine vicarious liability and to be able to use them in answering problem questions. It is also important to be able to comment on changes in the law.

Please read 'Working Under Cover' by Sarah Wilkinson, 2016, 166 NLJ 7698 p15 which explains and comments on the Supreme Court cases of *Cox v Ministry of Justice* [2016] and *Mohamud v Morrison Supermarkets plc* [2016].

## *Frolic of their own*

The employer will not be liable for a tort committed by an employee when the employee is on 'a frolic of his own' (*Joel v Morrison* (1834) 6 C&P 501). This will be seen as outside the course of employment. One factor which is taken into account is whether the employee is doing something for his own purposes rather than for his employer. It may be an employee driving off route in his employer's vehicle.

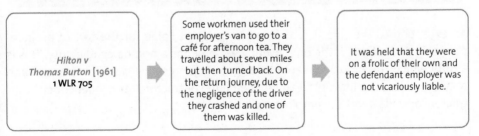

Hilton v Thomas Burton [1961] 1 WLR 705 → Some workmen used their employer's van to go to a café for afternoon tea. They travelled about seven miles but then turned back. On the return journey, due to the negligence of the driver they crashed and one of them was killed. → It was held that they were on a frolic of their own and the defendant employer was not vicariously liable.

In contrast to the above decision, in *Harvey v O'Dell* [1958] 1 All ER 657 some workmen travelled five miles from their site for lunch. There was an accident and one of them was injured. There was no canteen on site. It was held that the journey was within the course of employment and the employer was liable.

## The employer's indemnity

The employer and employee are jointly liable for the tort which has been committed. The claimant may sue either of them but will nearly always sue the employer. The employer has a right of indemnity against the employee which means that they can reclaim any damages paid to the claimant from the employee. The employer may reclaim at common law under the principle in *Lister v Romford Ice* [1957] AC 555. A father and son both worked for the defendant. The son was employed as a lorry driver and he negligently knocked down his father. The father sued the defendant for negligence under the principle of vicarious liability. The defendant then sued the son claiming an indemnity for the damages paid to the father. The House of Lords held that the son was in breach of an implied term in his contract of employment that he would use reasonable care. The defendant employer was entitled to be paid back by the son.

After this case employers' insurers agreed not to use the right of indemnity to claim from employees. Only in exceptional circumstances, for example, a deliberate and malicious act would this right be used.

## Independent contractors

If an independent contractor commits a tort while carrying out work for an employer, the employer is not liable. The independent contractor is liable for their own torts.

### Common Pitfall

When answering a problem question on vicarious liability if you decide that someone, who for example, commits a negligent act is not an employee but an independent contractor, then the employer will not be vicariously liable. Remember to consider that then it is the independent contractor who is liable for their own negligent act.

An exception to the rule that the employer is not liable for the tort of an independent contractor is if the employer owes someone a non-delegable duty. This is a duty which the employer cannot delegate legal responsibility for even though they can delegate the work to an independent contractor. If the independent contractor commits a tort the employer will be liable.

In *Bottomley v Todmorden Cricket Club* [2003] EWCA Civ 1575 the cricket club organised a fireworks event which was put on by an independent contractor. The claimant, who was helping the independent contractor was injured and neither of them had insurance. The cricket club was held liable as they had failed to check the independent contractor was competent or that they had insurance.

*Woodland v Essex CC* [2013] **UKSC 66**  A school contracted out swimming lessons to an independent contractor. The independent contractor failed to notice the ten year old claimant was in difficulties in the swimming pool during a lesson and she suffered brain damage.  The Supreme Court held that the school owed a non-delegable duty to the pupil for activities which were part of the curriculum and carried out during school hours and the school remained liable.

## Putting it into practice

Read the question below and attempt an outline answer.

Ian owns a private prison and employs Jess and Kamal as prison officers. Liz, a nurse, runs her own private practice visiting patients in their homes but she also regularly works at the prison. She is paid a fixed fee per day but Ian does not deduct tax. When on duty in the prison she wears a prison nurses' uniform and all medical equipment and medicines are provided by Ian. One day Liz was on duty in the prison hospital attending Marco, a sick prisoner. Liz misread his medical records and gave him the wrong medicine which caused him to suffer brain damage.

A few days later Jess was escorting a prisoner to his cell. She was standing at the bottom of a flight of stairs. Nick, another prisoner, had just been washing the floor on an upper landing and was standing at the top of the same flight of stairs carrying a mop and a metal bucket filled with water. He carelessly dropped the bucket which hit Jess and broke her arm.

Kamal works as a driver transporting prisoners. Ian lends Kamal to LockUUp, who also transport prisoners, for a few weeks. During this time Kamal is paid by Ian, wears his normal uniform and drives his usual prison van but he is given daily instructions by LockUUp. While picking up a prisoner from court Kamal has an argument with Oli, a court official, over the paperwork and punches Oli in the face breaking his nose.

**Advise Marco, Jess and Oli of any claims they may make in tort in respect of the above incidents.**

## Outline answer – vicarious liability, employees and independent contractors, torts, akin to employees, course of employment

❖ *Marco v Ian/Liz*

  ❖ Vicarious liability: three factors to establish: a tort, committed by an employee.
  ❖ Committed in the course of employment. Giving Marco the wrong medicine is negligence, *Century Insurance v Northern Ireland Road Transport Board*.
  ❖ Is Liz an employee or akin to an employee? Using *Ready Mixed Concrete v Minister of Pensions* she has her own patients and pays her own tax which would suggest she is an independent contractor. However, she wears a uniform, is provided with equipment and receives regular pay which would make her an employee.
  ❖ As she works at the prison regularly could she be integrated into the organisation? Ian also has some control over her as he can tell her what to do.
  ❖ If she is not an employee using these tests consider if she in a relationship akin to employment. *JGE v Trustees of Portsmouth RC Diocese*; she is presumably accountable to Ian for her work; and looking after the prisoners' health is a central part of the organisation; it could be argued she is in a relationship akin to an employee; act is while she is working, so in course of employment.
  ❖ A further argument following *Woodland v Essex* is that looking after vulnerable people is a non-delegable duty and if that applies Ian remains liable.

❖ *Jess v Ian/Nick*

  ❖ Vicarious liability: Nick is negligent in dropping the bucket.

- ❖ Is Nick an employee? Not in the traditional sense but is he akin to an employee? In *Cox v Ministry of Justice* two factors were relevant to decide; was the work integral to the business and the risk of committing a tort. Cleaning the prison is part of running it and it creates the risk so Nick could be akin to an employee.
- ❖ But is he paid? If not his case could be distinguished from *Cox*.
- ❖ If he is regarded as akin to an employee is he acting in the course of employment? He is carrying the bucket for work.
- ❖ If Ian was not liable Jess could sue Nick for negligence but is unlikely to obtain any damages.

❖ *Oli v Ian/LockUUp*

- ❖ Vicarious liability: Kamal punching Oli is the tort of battery.
- ❖ The question tells us Kamal is an employee of Ian but has been lent to LockUUp; originally the courts chose one employer but following *Viasystems v Thermal Transfer* it is possible to have dual vicarious liability.
- ❖ While it appears Ian retains most control, LockUUp also have a right of control and as Kamal has worked for them for a period of time he could be seen as integrated into their business.
- ❖ Is Kamal acting in the course of employment? The close connection test from *Lister v Hesley Hall* applies, is there a close connection between the tort and the job?
- ❖ In *Mohamud v Morrison Supermarkets plc* the Supreme Court said two things were needed, a relationship between the defendant and the wrongdoer and, second, a connection between that relationship and the act.
- ❖ Here Kamal is an employee and, second, his job was to collect and transport prisoners which is what he was doing. There is a strong case that both Ian and LockUUp are vicariously liable.

# Table of key cases referred to in this chapter

| Key case | Area of law | Principle |
|---|---|---|
| *Cox v Ministry of Justice* [2016] UKSC 10 | Prison catering manager injured by prisoner dropping bag of rice. Prison vicariously liable. | The two important factors were the activity was integral to work of prison and it created a risk of harm. |
| *Hilton v Thomas Burton* [1961] 1 WLR 705 | Workmen travelled seven miles for tea and one was killed in a road accident. Employer was not vicariously liable. | If someone is on a frolic of their own this is outside the course of employment and the employer is not liable. |

| Key case | Area of law | Principle |
|---|---|---|
| *Lister v Hesley Hall* [2001] 2 All ER 769 | A warden sexually abused boys at a boarding school. The House of Lords held the school was vicariously liable. | The second Salmond test was replaced by the test of a 'close connection' between the tort and the job. |
| *Lloyd v Grace, Smith & Co* [1912] AC 716 | A solicitor's clerk fraudulently transferred a client's house to himself. | The solicitors firm was vicariously liable because they held the clerk out as having authority. |
| *Mersey Docks and Harbour Board v Coggins & Griffiths* [1947] AC 1 | MDHB lent a driver and crane to C&G. The driver injured someone. House of Lords held MDHB still liable as they paid him and could dismiss. | If lending an employee the employer with most control is liable. (But see the effect of *Viasystems*.) |
| *Mohamud v Morrison Supermarkets plc* [2016] UKSC 11 | An employee at a petrol station assaulted a customer. He was serving a customer and his acts were connected to this. The employer was vicariously liable. | The Supreme Court said there are two factors to establish a sufficient connection: the nature of the job and a close connection between the act and the job. |
| *Ready Mixed Concrete v Minister of Pensions* [1968] 2 QB 497 | The drivers bought the lorries and took the risk of loss. The drivers were independent contractors not employees. | The economic reality test uses a range of factors to decide if someone is an employee. |
| *Rose v Plenty* [1976] 1 WLR 141 | A milkman paid a 13 year old boy to help him although he had been told not to have anyone on his milk float. The boy was injured helping and the employer was vicariously liable. | The prohibited act was for the employer's benefit. |
| *Various Claimants v Catholic Child Welfare Society* [2013] UKSC 56 | Boys at a boarding school were sexually abused by Brothers who worked for the Institute. | The Institute was vicariously liable as the Brothers were in a relationship akin to employees and there was a close connection between their acts and their work. |
| *Viasystems v Thermal Transfer* [2005] EWCA Civ 1151 | S, a fitter, worked for CAT and was also supervised by D Ltd. He caused a flood in a factory. | S was integrated into both businesses and both had a right of control. There was dual vicarious liability for D Ltd and CAT. |

@ Visit the book's companion website to test your knowledge

❖ Resources include a subject map, revision tip podcasts, downloadable diagrams, MCQ quizzes for each chapter and a flashcard glossary

❖ www.routledge.com/cw/optimizelawrevision

# 9

# Defamation and Privacy

## Revision objectives

**Understand the law**
- Can you define libel and slander and explain the differences between them?
- Can you outline the three requirements to establish defamation?
- Can you list the nine defences to defamation?
- Define the rights under Article 8 and Article 10 of the European Convention on Human Rights?
- Explain the duty of confidence and the right of privacy?

**Remember the details**
- Can you explain the three requirements for defamation using cases to illustrate your answer?
- Can you explain the single publication rule under s8 Defamation Act 2013?
- Can you explain the defences available under the Defamation Act 2013?
- Can you explain the cases of *Campbell v MGN* and *PJS v Newsgroup Newspapers Ltd*?

**Reflect critically on areas of debate**
- Can you explain the requirement of serious harm under s1 Defamation Act 2013 and how it can be established?
- Can you discuss how the courts balance Article 8 and Article 10 rights?

**Contextualise**
- Do you understand the overall effect of the Defamation Act 2013 in favour of freedom of speech over the right to privacy?
- Do you understand the problems faced by the courts in controlling defamation on social media?

**Apply your skills and knowledge**
- Can you write an outline answer to the question at the end of this chapter?

# Chapter Map

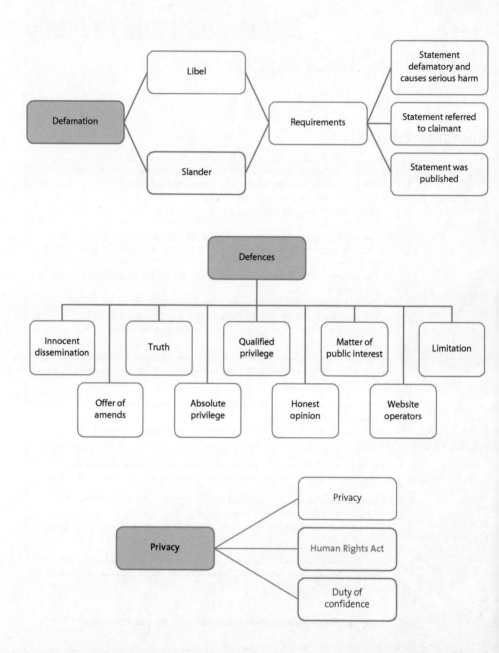

# Introduction

The tort of defamation protects a person's reputation. Defamation must be considered along with the rules on privacy including Article 8, the right to private life, and Article 10, the right to freedom of expression, from the European Convention on Human Rights which was incorporated into English law by the Human Rights Act 1998 and the duty of confidence.

Defamation cases used to be tried by jury but the Defamation Act 2013 s11 provides that defamation trials will be without a jury unless the court orders otherwise. In *Yeo v Times Newspapers* [2015] EWHC 2132 the claimant, a Member of Parliament, was secretly recorded by a journalist saying he could act for him. Later two articles in the newspapers alleged he had agreed to take payment from a company in breach of the MPs' Code of Conduct. The newspaper claimed trial by jury on the basis of a public interest but the court refused. 'Parliament no longer regards jury trial as a right of "the highest importance" in defamation cases' (Warby J).

A claim for defamation must be brought within one year from the date on which the right of action accrued Limitation Act 1980 s4A as amended by the Defamation Act 1996 s5(2).

If a claim for defamation is brought against someone who is not domiciled in the UK or EU the court does not have jurisdiction to hear the case unless England and Wales is the most appropriate place (Defamation Act 2013 s9). The aim is to stop people using the English courts for defamatory statements made elsewhere.

A claim for defamation ends with the death of the claimant or the defendant (Law Reform (Miscellaneous Provisions) Act 1934 s1(1)).

# Comparisons between libel and slander

| Libel | Slander |
|---|---|
| A statement in a permanent form, e.g. writing, picture, statue, film, theatre (Theatres Act 1968 s4), radio and television (Broadcasting Act 1990 s166) | A statement in a temporary form e.g. spoken, gesture |
| Civil wrong Criminal offence if it leads to a breach of the peace | Civil wrong only |
| Must prove serious harm to reputation | Must prove serious harm to reputation But also must prove 'special damage' which is financial loss except in the following two cases, any statement that: (1) the claimant committed a crime punishable by imprisonment; or (2) the claimant is unfit for any office, profession, calling, trade or business |

# Elements of defamation

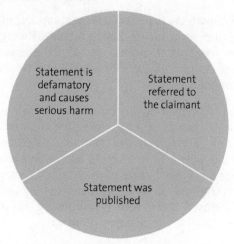

## The statement is defamatory and causes serious harm

There have been various attempts to define what makes a statement defamatory but no complete definition has been agreed. In *Sim v Stretch* [1936] 52 TLR 669 it was defined as:

'the publication of an untrue statement which lowers the claimant in the estimation of right thinking members of society or causes them to be shunned or avoided.'

It is a statement which harms someone's reputation, for example, a false statement that someone is a terrorist would be defamatory.

One test of what is defamatory was set out by Lord Atkin in *Sim v Stretch* [1936]:

'would the words tend to lower the plaintiff in the estimation of right thinking members of society generally?'

The Defamation Act 2013 s1(1) provides that 'A statement is not defamatory unless its publication has caused or is likely to cause serious harm to the reputation of the claimant.' Under s1(2) in the case of a body that trades for a profit it must be shown 'it has caused or is likely to cause the body serious financial loss'.

The additional requirement of serious harm means that minor cases or technical defamations can no longer be taken to court.

The test for 'right thinking members of society' is an objective standard of the reasonable person.

Byrne v Deane [1937] 2 All ER 204 → A member of a golf club told the police about an illegal gambling machine in the club. A notice then appeared in the club which read, 'But he who gave the game away, may he byrne in hell and rue the day'. The claimant sued for defamation. → It was held that telling the police about an illegal machine would not lower the claimant in the eyes of right thinking members of the public. The statement was not defamatory.

If someone is rude or abusive this is not defamatory. In *Berkoff v Burchill* [1996] 4 All ER 1008 the defendant described the claimant as 'hideous looking'. It was held that as the claimant made his living as an actor this was capable of lowering him in the eyes of the public.

## Innuendo

Words or pictures which appear innocent may sometimes have a hidden meaning (or double meaning). If some people know this hidden meaning it will make the statement defamatory. In *Tolley v Fry* [1931] AC 333 the claimant was an amateur golfer, which meant he was not paid. The defendants published an advertisement with a picture of the claimant playing golf and a bar of the defendant's chocolate sticking out of his pocket. Although this did not appear defamatory people who knew the claimant would think he had been paid for the advertisement and this would damage his reputation as an amateur golfer.

## Serious harm

The requirement of serious harm is to prevent trivial claims being brought. In *Cooke v MGN* [2014] EWHC 2831 (QB) following a television programme, *Benefits Street* which looked at people living on state benefits, the defendant published a newspaper article under the heading, 'Millionaire Tory cashes in on TV Benefits Street'. The article stated that the claimants were making big profits renting poor quality housing to people on social security. The following week they published an apology and said it was a mistake. It was held that although the statements were true they were defamatory because people would think less of them. However, distress or injury to feelings was not enough to establish serious harm.

Bean J said that evidence of serious harm was not needed if a statement would obviously cause such harm and he gave the example of a false statement in a national newspaper that someone was 'a terrorist or paedophile'.

In *Smith v Unknown Defendant* [2016] EWHC 1775 the defendant operates a website but their real name and location are hidden. In May 2016 an article appeared on the website which falsely stated that 'Smith is a paedophile and child rapist' and a 'known child molester' along with false photographs of the claimant naked having sex with other men. The claimant complained to the operator of the website under s5 Defamation Act 2013 but this was met with abuse. The claimant runs a business and under s1(2) it must be shown that publication would cause 'serious financial loss'. It was held that the claimant's reputation will have been substantially harmed and he was awarded damages and an injunction requiring removal of the material.

## The statement referred to the claimant

A statement which names or has a photograph of the claimant meets this requirement. If the claimant is not named, the test is whether a reasonable person who knows the facts would believe that the words referred to the claimant. To succeed in a defamation claim there is no need to show that the defendant intended to defame the claimant, it can happen by chance.

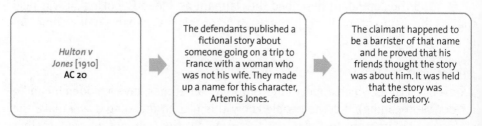

Even if a statement is true about one person it may still be defamatory of another. In *Newstead v London Express Newspaper Ltd* [1940] 1 KB 377 the defendant published a true report that Harold Newstead, a 30 year old barman from Camberwell, had been convicted of bigamy. The claimant, a hairdresser, was about the same age and lived in Camberwell. The claimant proved that people who knew him believed it was him.

The problem caused in this case could be avoided by giving the address of the person named in the article.

If a defamatory statement is made about a large group of people an individual member of that group will not be able to sue, for example, 'All politicians are crooks'. If the statement is about a small group then each individual could sue (*Knuppfer v London Express Newspaper Ltd* [1944] AC 116).

# The statement was published

This requirement does not mean that the statement was published in the normal sense of being published in a book or a newspaper. It simply means that the statement was made to a third party, that is, someone apart from the claimant.

## Spouses

- ❖ If the defendant tells their husband or wife – that is not publication.
- ❖ If the defendant tells the claimant's husband or wife – that is publication.
- ❖ If the defendant sends a defamatory letter to the claimant that is not publication as it is not published to a third party.
- ❖ But what if the letter is opened by someone else? The courts apply a test to determine whether it was reasonably foreseeable that someone else would read the letter.

In *Theaker v Richardson* [1962] 1 All ER 229 the defendant wrote a defamatory letter to the claimant and put it in a brown, sealed envelope. The letter was opened by the claimant's husband who thought it was an election leaflet. It was held by the Court of Appeal that the husband's action was foreseeable and it was publication.

In contrast to this decision in *Huth v Huth* [1915] 2 KB 32 the defendant sent a defamatory letter to his wife, which was opened and read by the butler. It was not part of the butler's duties to open letters addressed to his employer and this was not foreseeable. It was held not to be publication.

## The internet

If defamatory material is posted on the internet the author will be the publisher. The internet service provider plays a passive role in providing the service and will not normally be regarded as a publisher. Compare the following two cases.

| Godfrey v Demon Internet [2001] QB 201 | Tamiz v Google [2013] EWCA Civ 68 |
| --- | --- |
| The claimant asked the defendant to remove a defamatory article which had been posted on their server but the defendant did not remove it for ten days. It was held that the defendant was liable for that period of time. They could not rely on the defence of innocent dissemination under s1 of the Defamation Act 1996 because they knew about it. | The defendant was not responsible for defamatory comments on a blog about the claimant. When the defendant was told about them it informed the blogger who removed the comments a few days later. The court said that the defendant may have been treated as a 'publisher' if they had done nothing. The defendant was not liable. |

The original common law rule was that every new publication was a new defamation. This is a particular problem with a defamation posted on a website because each time someone accessed it this created a new defamation. This rule was changed by the Defamation Act 2013 s8 which provides for a single publication rule. If someone publishes a defamation and later they publish substantially the same statement, then the time limit for bringing a claim for the second statement is one year from the time of the first publication.

This rule does not apply if the manner of the later publication is materially different from the first publication, for example, the first publication is a few lines in a local newspaper and the later one is a prominent article in a national newspaper.

## Aim Higher

Essay questions on defamation frequently ask for some criticism or evaluation of the law. Read the following article, 'Tilting at Windmills', by A Mullis and A Scott, 2014, 77 Modern Law Review 1 pp87–109.

Prepare an outline answer identifying the changes made by the **Defamation Act 2013** and some comment on whether they have improved and clarified the law.

## Defences

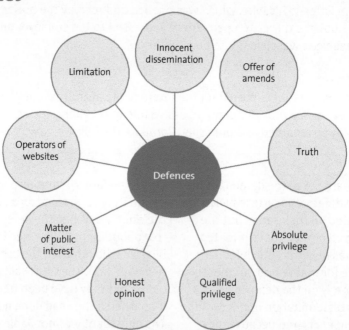

### Innocent dissemination

This was originally a common law defence but is now contained in the Defamation Act 1996 s1. The defence protects the mechanical distributors, for example, the printers and sellers of the defamatory material.

Section 1(1), the defendant must show that they:

(a) are not the author, editor or publisher;
(b) took reasonable care in relation to its publication;
(c) did not know and had no reason to believe that what they did caused or contributed to the publication of a defamatory statement.

The section also provides that anyone involved in printing, copying, distributing or the broadcaster of a live programme with no control over the maker of the statement or the operator of a communications system used to transmit the statement will not be regarded as an author, editor or publisher. In *Godfrey v Demon Internet* [2001] the defendants could not rely on s1 because they knew about the defamatory statement on their server but failed to remove it for ten days and could not show that they had taken reasonable care.

## Offer of amends

If the defamation has been made unintentionally the Defamation Act 1996 ss2–4 provides a defence of 'offer to make amends'. It covers situations where the publisher believes that the statement is true but it is false or that the statement is true about one person but is defamatory of another, for example, *Newstead v London Express Newspaper* [1940]. It provides a mechanism for the parties to reach an agreement over the defamation without going to court.

Section 2, the defendant must:

❖ make an offer in writing to publish a correction and apology in a reasonable manner; and
❖ pay the claimant compensation and costs.

Section 3 provides that if the offer is accepted the claimant cannot bring proceedings for defamation.

Section 4 provides that if the offer is not accepted the fact that the offer was made is a defence to a defamation claim.

## Truth

The previous common law defence of justification has been abolished by s2 of the Defamation Act 2013 and replaced by the defence of truth. Section 2(1) 'It is a defence … for the defendant to show that the imputation conveyed by the statement complained of is substantially true.'

Section 2(3) provides that if the statement contains two or more implications and one or more are not substantially true the defence of truth does not fail if those which are not true do not seriously harm the claimant's reputation.

If the defendant can prove that the statement is substantially true that provides a complete defence. This can be illustrated by the old case of *Alexander v North*

*Eastern Railway Co* (1865) 29 JP 692. The defendant put a notice on the station noticeboard that the claimant had been convicted of travelling without a ticket and fined £1 or three weeks' imprisonment if he failed to pay. The actual sentence was £1 or two weeks' imprisonment. It was held that the defence of justification succeeded as the statement was substantially true.

## Absolute privilege

In some circumstances the right to freedom of speech is so important that a person making an untrue statement will not be liable for defamation. This applies even if the statement is made maliciously, knowing it is wrong. This defence allows people to carry out their work without the worry that they could be sued for defamation. Examples include MPs speaking in the House of Commons and witnesses giving evidence in court.

| Parliament | The courts | The Executive |
|---|---|---|
| • Bill of Rights 1688 proceedings in Parliament cannot be questioned in any court outside Parliament.<br>• This covers debates in Parliament, committees, witnesses.<br>• Reports ordered to be published by Parliament, e.g. Hansard.<br>• It does not cover statements by MPs outside Parliament. | • Privilege includes statements made in courts, tribunals and similar bodies such as the General Medical Council; it covers judges, lawyers, witnesses.<br>• Statements made to lawyers for the purpose of proceedings.<br>• Fair and accurate reports of proceedings made soon afterwards. | • Privilege covers statements made by Government ministers to other ministers.<br>• It does not cover statements by civil servants. |

In *A v UK* [2003] All ER (D) 264 an MP in Parliament described the claimant as the 'neighbour from Hell' and gave her name and address. As a result she had to move house. She claimed breach of Article 6 the right to a fair trial. It was held that statements in Parliament were protected by absolute privilege and it was not a breach of Article 6.

## Qualified privilege

This defence applies to a wider range of situations than absolute privilege. An important limitation on the defence is that the statement has to be made without malice and with a belief in its truth.

### At common law

There are two requirements:

❖ the person making the statement must have a legal, moral or social duty to make it; and

❖ the person receiving the statement must have a corresponding duty to receive it.

---

**Case precedent – *Watt v Longsdon* [1930] 1 KB 130**

**Facts:** L was the liquidator of a company with a branch in Morocco. W was managing director in Morocco and B was a manager. B sent a letter to L stating that W was often drunk and immoral. L sent a copy of the letter to S, the chairman of the company and to Mrs W. The allegations were untrue.

**Principle:** It was held by the Court of Appeal that the:

(i) Letter from B to L: was covered by qualified privilege as both had a common interest in the company.
(ii) Letter from L to S: was also covered; there was a duty to tell S and a duty to receive it as both were employed by the company.
(iii) Letter to Mrs W: no moral or social duty to tell her about unfounded gossip and the defence of qualified privilege failed.

**Application:** The courts have been reluctant to set out definitive rules on when the above principles apply. One example is an employer giving a reference for an employee. It is important in problem questions to consider if there is a duty on the party making the statement and on the party receiving it for the defence of qualified privilege to succeed.

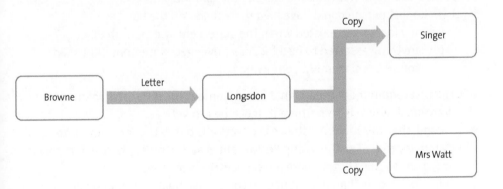

## Under statute

Under the Defamation Act 1996 s15 Schedule 1 the following are privileged if made without malice:

❖ Fair reports of proceedings in Parliament, for example, in a newspaper.
❖ Fair reports of court cases which are not made at the time.
❖ Fair reports of Government inquiries and international organisations.

Under Schedule 2 the following are privileged if made without malice and the claimant has been given the chance to comment:

❖ Reports of public meetings of councils, companies and other public bodies.

Under the Defamation Act 2013 s6 publication of a statement in a scientific or academic journal is privileged if two conditions are met:

❖ the statement relates to a scientific or academic matter;
❖ before publication an independent peer review of the statement has been carried out by the editor and another expert.

Under s6(6) the defence fails if it is shown it was made with malice.

This defence allows academic criticisms to be made but is limited to statements in academic journals.

## Honest opinion

This is a defence that the person making the statement honestly held that opinion. Its purpose is to encourage free speech. The defence replaces the common law defence of fair comment.

Under s3 Defamation Act 2013 three conditions must be satisfied:

S3(2)  the statement was a statement of opinion;
S3(3)  the statement indicated the basis of the opinion; and
S3(4)  an honest person could have held the opinion on the basis of
    (a) any fact which existed when the statement was published; or
    (b) anything asserted to be a fact in a privileged statement published before the statement complained of.

❖ The first requirement means that the statement must be an opinion rather than a fact, which is something that can be proved.
❖ Second, the statement must give the facts it is based on. For example, a statement that, 'The Buttercup Restaurant is awful' must give the fact this is based on, because of the food, the service, the prices etc.
❖ Third, in deciding if an honest person could have held that opinion an objective test is applied; there is no need for the opinion to be reasonable as long as it is honestly held.
❖ A privileged statement is a statement covered by one of the defences of absolute privilege, qualified privilege, public interest or a peer reviewed journal.

Under s3(5) the defence will fail if it is shown that the defendant did not hold that opinion.

## Publication on a matter of public interest

The previous Reynolds defence at common law has been replaced by s4 Defamation Act 2013. It is a defence to show that:

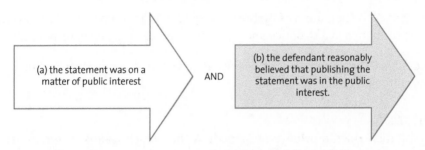

(a) the statement was on a matter of public interest

AND

(b) the defendant reasonably believed that publishing the statement was in the public interest.

The first requirement of public interest is very wide and is not confined to political issues. The second requirement involves a subjective test whether the defendant had the belief and the court then makes an objective judgment whether that belief was reasonable.

In *Flood v Times Newspapers Ltd* [2012] UKSC 11 the defendant published in its newspaper and on its website an article naming the claimant, under the heading, 'Detective accused of taking bribes from Russian exiles' in connection with extradition. The police investigated the matter but found no evidence against the claimant. He sued for libel and the defendant claimed qualified privilege. The Supreme Court said that Article 8 rights to privacy had to be balanced against Article 10 rights to publish. The defendant had done enough to check the information which was from an anonymous source and it was also in the public interest to publish that information. The defence of qualified privilege succeeded. Cases such as *Flood* which were before the Defamation Act 2013 will still be used as guidance in interpreting s4 although they are not binding.

Section 4(5) provides that the defence applies to both statements of fact and opinion.

## Operators of websites

Under s5 Defamation Act 2013 a new defence has been introduced for operators of websites due to the problems caused by people posting defamatory comments on websites.

S5(1) This defence applies if an action is brought against the operator of a website for a statement posted on the website.

S5(2) It is a defence to show that it was not the operator who posted the statement.

S5(3) The defence will fail if the claimant shows the following:

(a) It was not possible for the claimant to identify the person who posted the statement,

(b) The claimant gave a notice of complaint to the operator, and

(c) The operator failed to respond to the complaint in accordance with the regulations.

The Defamation (Operators of Websites) Regulations 2013 provide details on what must be contained in a s5 notice and what the operator must do in response.

It is possible to bring proceedings against an unknown defendant by posting documents on their website.

## Limitation

The limitation rules provide time periods within which claims in tort must be brought. Under s5(2) of the Defamation Act 1996 in claims for defamation no action shall be brought after one year from when the cause of action accrued.

In addition under s8 Defamation Act 2013 the single publication rule provides that if there is a subsequent publication of the defamatory statement the right of action runs from the date of the first publication.

## Summary of defences

| Defence | Explanation | Effect |
|---|---|---|
| Innocent dissemination Defamation Act 1996 s1 | Distributors: took reasonable care; and did not know it was defamatory | Protects distributors and also covers live broadcasts |
| Offer of amends Defamation Act 1996 s2 | Unintentional defamation and believe it is true or it is true about one person | If not accepted by claimant it is a defence |
| Truth Defamation Act 2013 s2 | Substantially true | A complete defence |
| Absolute privilege | Statements in and reports of Parliament, Courts, Government | May be made maliciously A complete defence |
| Qualified privilege: *Common law* Defamation Act 1996 s15 Defamation Act 2013 s6 | Duty to make and to receive Later reports Parliament, Courts, Government Peer reviewed journals | All must be without malice |
| Honest opinion Defamation Act 2013 s3 | Must be an opinion not a fact | Fails if defendant did not have the opinion |
| Publication on matter of public interest Defamation Act 2013 s4 | Must be a matter of public interest *and* must have reasonable belief it is in public interest to publish | Covers statements on a wide range of issues |

| Websites Defamation Act 2013 s5 | Protects operator if someone else posted it | Defence fails if operator is told and fails to act in time |
| --- | --- | --- |
| Limitation Defamation Act 1996 s5(2) Defamation Act 2013 s8 | Must sue within one year Second publication sue in one year from original defamation | Short time limit Restricts claims for repetition of the same defamation |

# Remedies

The two main remedies for defamation are damages and injunctions (see Chapter 10).

Interim injunctions are also important in defamation and privacy cases (see Privacy: Remedies). In *Barron v Vines* [2016] EWHC 1226 QB the claimants were Labour MPs in Rotherham where the defendant was also a UKIP councillor. During an interview on national television news, the defendant said that the claimants knew about the widespread sexual abuse of children in Rotherham but did nothing about it. This was untrue. The claimants were re-elected in the General Election. The court said that caution had to be used in deciding compensation where one politician libelled another on a matter of public interest. In balancing the claimants' reputations and the right to freedom of speech the court awarded them £40,000 damages each.

# Privacy
## Introduction
There are three areas to consider privacy, human rights and the duty of confidence which are interrelated. The law in this area is still developing and a number of points have yet to be clarified by the courts.

Privacy → Human rights → Duty of confidence

## Privacy
The idea of privacy as a legal right has been debated for many years. The tort of defamation protects someone from false statements made about them but should someone be protected from disclosure of true information about them? Do people have a right to a private life? This has been a problem for celebrities being photographed coming out of night clubs, meetings of Alcoholics Anonymous, brothels or simply going about their daily lives.

One example is *Kaye v Robertson* [1991] FSR 62 in which the claimant, a famous television actor, was injured in an accident and taken to hospital. The defendant was a photographer from a newspaper who went into the hospital and took photographs of the claimant asleep in bed. He also falsely claimed that the claimant had given him permission to interview him. The Court of Appeal stated that there was no right of privacy in English law. The court relied on the tort of malicious falsehood which was the fact that the defendant knew he had not been given permission. An injunction was granted to stop the defendants publishing this false statement but the court could not stop them publishing the photograph or a slightly amended article.

In *PJS v News Group Newspapers Ltd* [2016] UKSC 26 the Supreme Court has further developed the tort of privacy. In that case Lord Mance said that publication of private sexual encounters will constitute the tort of invasion of privacy. The right of privacy took account not just of revealing private information but also of the effect of intrusion (see facts of the case in Remedies below). In this respect it is wider than the duty of confidence.

## Human Rights Act 1998

The Human Rights Act 1998 incorporated the European Convention on Human Rights into English law. Two of the important articles are Article 8 and Article 10.

### Right to respect for private life

Article 8(1) Everyone has the right to respect for his private and family life, his home and his correspondence.

8(2) There shall be no interference by a public authority with the exercise of this right except such as is in accordance with the law and is necessary in a democratic society in the interests of national security, public safety or the economic well-being of the country, for the prevention of disorder or crime, for the protection of health or morals, or for the protection of the rights and freedoms of others.

### Freedom of expression

Article 10(1) Everyone has the right to freedom of expression. This right shall include freedom to hold opinions and to receive and impart information and ideas without interference by public authority...

10(2) The exercise of these freedoms ... may be subject to formalities, conditions, restrictions and penalties as are prescribed by law and are necessary in a democratic society ... for the protection of the reputation or rights of others.

Public bodies are bound by the rights under the Convention but Articles 8 and 10 also apply in disputes involving individuals.

In balancing the above two rights s12 Human Rights Act 1998 must be taken into account. It provides that if a court is considering granting relief it should consider how this might affect the right to freedom of expression. This was an important factor in granting an interim injunction in *PJS v News Group Newspapers Ltd* [2016].

## The duty of confidence

The common law recognises that in certain circumstances a duty of confidence may arise. It is probably based on the equitable obligation to respect confidential information and it is not a claim in tort. Originally it was necessary to establish a confidential relationship between the two parties, for example, doctor and patient but this requirement was changed in *Campbell*.

The requirements for a duty of confidence to arise are:

❖ The information must be of a private nature.
❖ It must be given in circumstances which impose an obligation of confidence.
❖ It is a breach if an unauthorised person sees the information.

### Case precedent – *Campbell v MGN* [2004] UKHL 22

**Facts:** Naomi Campbell was photographed leaving a meeting of Narcotics Anonymous. The defendants published the picture along with an article about her battle with drug addiction. First, was Naomi Campbell's attendance at NA meetings confidential? The test was whether a person would have a reasonable expectation the information would be kept confidential. The fact someone was being treated for drug addiction would be confidential. Second, Naomi Campbell had publicly stated that she did not take drugs, making it a public issue and not confidential. However, this did not mean that everything about her treatment was a public matter.

**Principle:** The court said that the test for establishing a duty of confidence was whether a person had a reasonable expectation of privacy in respect of the particular matter. The court had to balance the Article 8 right to privacy and the Article 10 right to freedom of expression. Because the claimant was receiving medical treatment for her addiction her right to privacy prevailed.

**Application:** This case changed the test for a duty of confidence from one based on a relationship to one based on reasonable expectation. There is now a two-stage test: first, is the information of a private nature? Second, if it is, it is necessary to balance the right to private life, against the right to freedom of expression. In doing this the courts take all the circumstances into account so, for example, if it involves a public figure and relates to their public work this may tilt the balance towards disclosure.

## Remedies

The main remedies are damages and injunctions.

### Injunctions

If someone wants to stop the information being made public they can apply for an interim injunction which is issued before trial. However, the courts have to keep in mind the right to freedom of expression under Article 10. In addition s12(3) of the Human Rights Act 1998 provides that such relief should not be granted 'unless the court is satisfied that the applicant is likely to establish that publication should not be allowed'.

The effect is that it is very difficult to obtain an interim injunction. However, in the following case the Supreme Court has created a tort of invasion of privacy and granted an interim injunction. In *PJS v News Group Newspapers Ltd* [2016] a celebrity who was married with young children had sex with another couple. The couple sold the story to the defendants who intended to publish it. The celebrity sued for misuse of private information and breach of confidence.

The High Court granted an injunction for 11 weeks. The story was then published in the United States and on the internet.

The Court of Appeal then set the injunction aside on the basis that the information had been made public and the injunction restricted the defendant's rights under Article 10.

The Supreme Court said that the Court of Appeal had made an error in balancing Articles 8 and 10 by stating that s12 Human Rights Act 1998 gave more weight to Article 10, when the articles were of equal weight. Public interest in the sex life of celebrities could not by itself outweigh the celebrity's right to privacy. Disclosing private sexual encounters would be the tort of invasion of privacy. The Court of Appeal had not realised the difference between information on the internet and the much greater intrusive effect if disclosed in the English media. This would have a great effect on the children. Further disclosure would be an invasion of his, his partner's and his children's right to privacy. The interim injunction could continue until the trial.

## Up for Debate

Read the judgment of Lord Mance in *PJS v News Group Newspapers Ltd* [2016] in the Supreme Court.

Explain the relationship between Article 8 privacy and Article 10 freedom of expression.

Explain how the case has defined the tort of privacy.

# Putting it into practice

Read the scenario below and answer the question.

Pat is a lecturer in the medical school at Northern University. He went to the medical students' Christmas Ball, got drunk and fell asleep in the corner. Rose, a student, saw Pat lying on the floor and decided to play a joke on him. She undressed and then took all his clothes off. One of her friends used Rose's phone to take a picture of Rose lying next to Pat. The next day Rose emailed the Dean of the medical school stating, 'A fine example of the university staff! Drunk and has had sex with a student' and she attached the photograph. Rose also posted it along with her comments on the University Facebook page. Pat cannot remember anything about the Ball.

Sally the local Member of Parliament saw the post on the University Facebook page. A few days later she made a statement in the House of Commons that 'Pat organises drunken orgies with students at our local university. It needs to be investigated by the authorities.'

Pat had a research article published in the University journal about people returning from holiday with malaria, which could be spread if they were bitten by a UK bred mosquito. Tom, another member of staff, who disliked Pat wrote an article in the staff magazine which stated, 'Pat's research is flawed, it's only based on a small sample and it's just nonsense. He's an idiot.' Very few staff read the staff magazine.

**Advise Pat of any claims he may make in defamation.**

# Outline answer – defamation, libel and slander, requirements of the Defamation Act 2013, defences

❖ *Pat v Rose*

  ❖ Defamation: Libel: the email: the publication of a false statement which lowers the claimant in the eyes of right thinking members of society.
  ❖ There are two statements that he is drunk and has had sex with a student; right thinking members of society will think less of Pat probably on either count, *Byrne v Deane*.
  ❖ It refers to him as he is named and it has his photo.
  ❖ It is published as it is sent to the Dean.
  ❖ Has it caused or will it cause serious harm? Defamation Act 2013 s1. It would damage Pat's career.
  ❖ The Facebook post: it is defamatory; it refers to Pat; it is published to a wide audience; and will cause serious harm.

- ❖ Possible defences: truth s2 Defamation Act 2013, must show the statement is 'substantially true'; but here there are two allegations and the claim of sex could fail, and so would the defence.
- ❖ Section 4 Defamation Act 2013 publication on a matter of public interest: how universities are run and staff behave; but difficult for Rose to show she believed it was in the public interest to publish.
- ❖ Qualified privilege: is there a duty to tell and a duty to receive? There may be about Pat being drunk but it is a social occasion so may be not?
- ❖ Facebook: under s5 Defamation Act 2013 defence for website operator; but Pat could identify who posted it and we are not told Pat gave notice to the website operator.

❖ *Pat v Sally*

- ❖ Defamation: publication of a false statement which lowers the claimant in the eyes of right thinking members of society; it is slander as it is spoken; it is defamatory; it refers to him; it has been published as Sally made a statement in House of Commons; and is likely to cause Pat serious harm.
- ❖ For slander special damage must be proved, but not here as it implies Pat is unfit to do his job.
- ❖ Defences: absolute privilege; statements in Parliament are protected under the Bill of Rights 1688, *A v UK*, Sally has a complete defence.

❖ *Pat v Tom*

- ❖ Defamation: libel: is the statement defamatory? Calling his research nonsense is potentially defamatory; the statement he is an idiot may simply be abuse and is not covered; unless argued it is related to his research.
- ❖ It refers to him because he is named.
- ❖ It is published as it is in the staff journal, the fact few read it doesn't matter.
- ❖ It would cause serious harm saying he can't do research.
- ❖ Consider defences: honest opinion, s3 Defamation Act 2013, this may not be Tom's honest opinion as he dislikes Pat.
- ❖ Section 4 Defamation Act 2013 matter of public interest, but Tom probably cannot show reasonable belief in public interest to publish.
- ❖ Section 6 Defamation Act 2013 publication in an academic journal, relates to a scientific matter but has it been reviewed by the editor and another? Even if these conditions were met, Tom seems to have made the statement with malice which defeats the defence.

# Table of key cases referred to in this chapter

| Key case | Area of law | Principle |
|---|---|---|
| *Byrne v Deane* [1937] 2 All ER 204 | The claimant told the police of an illegal gambling machine at a golf club and a poem about him appeared on the noticeboard. | Right thinking members of society would not think worse of someone for telling the police of a crime. Even though members of the golf club would! |
| *Campbell v MGN* [2004] UKHL 22 | The defendant published a picture of the claimant leaving an Alcoholics Anonymous meeting and she claimed breach of the duty of confidence. | House of Lords held it was a breach of the duty of confidence. The Article 8 right of privacy took precedence over Article 10 freedom of speech as she was having treatment for alcoholism. |
| *Godfrey v Demon Internet* [2001] QB 201 | The claimant asked the defendant to remove a defamatory statement which had been posted on their server but the defendant did not do so for ten days. | The defendant could not rely on the defence of innocent dissemination under the Defamation Act 1996 s1 because they knew about the defamation. |
| *Hulton v Jones* [1910] AC 20 | The claimant's name was used in a made up story about someone going on holiday with a woman who was not his wife. | No need for intention in defamation. The claimant showed that his friends believed it was him, it referred to him and it was defamatory. |
| *PJS v News Group Newspapers* [2016] UKSC 26 | The defendants wanted to print an article about the married claimant's sex life. With private sexual matters private life took precedence over freedom of speech. | The Supreme Court said it was a breach of the tort of the right to privacy. An interim injunction was granted. |
| *Smith v Unknown Defendant* [2016] EWHC 1775 | A false statement that the claimant was a paedophile appeared on a website. He complained under s5 Defamation Act 2013. He traded for profit and had to show publication would cause serious financial loss under s2(1) Defamation Act 2013. | The court said his reputation would be substantially harmed and an injunction was granted to remove the material. |

| Key case | Area of law | Principle |
|---|---|---|
| *Theaker v Richardson* [1962] 1 All ER 229 | The defendant sent a defamatory letter to the claimant which was opened by her husband. | It was foreseeable this would happen and it was regarded as being published. |
| *Tolley v Fry* [1931] AC 333 | The defendant printed an advert with a picture of the claimant amateur golfer on it. He had a bar of Fry's chocolate sticking out of his pocket. | Although this did not seem defamatory those who knew him would think he was paid and think less of him. Defamation by innuendo. |
| *Watt v Longsdon* [1930] 1 KB 130 | L sent defamatory letters about W, a company employee, to the chairman of the company and to Mrs W. | The letter to the chairman was covered by qualified privilege. But there was no duty to tell Mrs W of gossip and this letter was defamatory. |

@ **Visit the book's companion website to test your knowledge**

❖ Resources include a subject map, revision tip podcasts, downloadable diagrams, MCQ quizzes for each chapter and a flashcard glossary

❖ www.routledge.com/cw/optimizelawrevision

## Revision objectives

**Understand the law**

- Can you identify what must be proved to establish contributory negligence and the effect of doing so?
- Can you identify what must be proved to establish consent and the effect of doing so?
- Can you outline the defence of illegality using a case to illustrate?
- Can you name the Act of Parliament dealing with limitation?

**Remember the details**

- Can you explain the standard that applies in determining if the claimant is contributory negligent and the exceptions to that standard?
- Can you explain the distinction from *Froom v Butcher* between the cause of the accident and the cause of the damage?
- Can you explain what is required to show that a claimant voluntarily consents to a risk?
- Can you explain why the defence of illegality failed in *Joyce v O'Brien*?
- Can you explain the different time periods for bringing claims in tort under the Limitation Act 1980?

**Reflect critically on areas of debate**

- Can you explain the circumstances in which children can be found contributorily negligent?
- Can you explain the effect of drinking alcohol on consent using cases to illustrate?
- Can you explain the principles on which the defence of illegality is based?

**Contextualise**

- Do you understand the relationship between the defences of contributory negligence and consent?
- Do you understand the relationship between contributory negligence and causation?
- Do you understand the difficulties the courts face in drawing a line between which illegal acts lead to the defence of illegality applying and which do not?

**Apply your skills and knowledge**

- Can you comment critically on the above three defences?
- Can you answer the question at the end of this chapter?

# Chapter Map

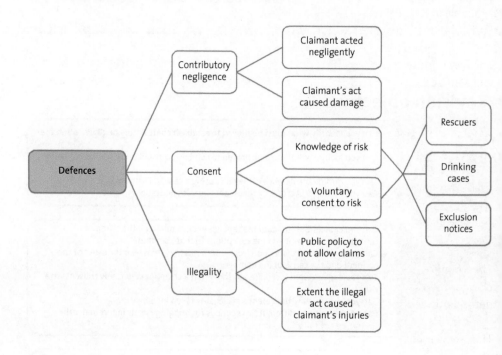

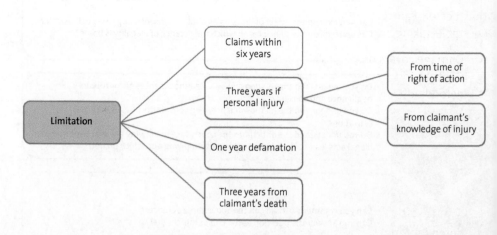

# Introduction

In any claim in tort the burden of proof is on the claimant to establish their case on a balance of probabilities. If the defendant raises a defence it is up to the defendant to establish that defence. This chapter will explain the general defences which are available in tort. These are in addition to the specific defences which are available for particular torts, for example, self-defence is available to a claim for battery.

The law imposes time limits for people bringing claims in tort and the rules on this will also be explained in the section on limitation.

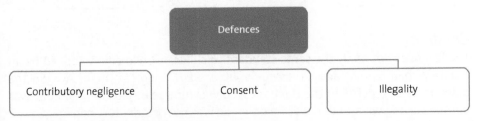

# Contributory negligence

The original common-law rule was that if the defendant could show that the claimant was partly to blame for the accident this was a complete defence and the defendant was not liable in negligence.

The law was changed by the Law Reform (Contributory Negligence) Act 1945 (hereinafter LR(CN) Act 1945) s1(1) which provides that if a person suffers harm partly through their own fault and partly through the fault of another, the damages which that person can recover will be reduced to the extent the court thinks 'just and equitable' taking into account the claimant's share in responsibility for the damage.

* Damage covers death, injury, property damage and economic loss.
* Contributory negligence is only a partial defence which means that the defendant will still have to pay some damages.

## Common Pitfall

Contributory negligence only applies to the claimant and not to any other party involved in an accident, for example, the defendant or a third party.

The defendant must prove:

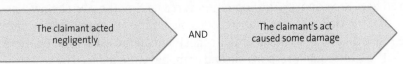

# The claimant acted negligently

It does not have to be shown that the claimant owes a duty of care in negligence to the defendant but simply that the claimant acted carelessly. The courts apply an objective standard to determine this.

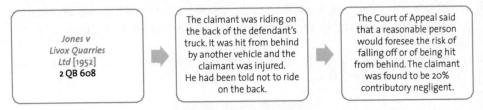

| Jones v Livox Quarries Ltd [1952] 2 QB 608 | → | The claimant was riding on the back of the defendant's truck. It was hit from behind by another vehicle and the claimant was injured. He had been told not to ride on the back. | → | The Court of Appeal said that a reasonable person would foresee the risk of falling off or of being hit from behind. The claimant was found to be 20% contributory negligent. |

## Children

The law does not apply the same standard to children. Children are judged by an ordinary child of that age. In *Yachuk v Oliver Blais & Co Ltd* [1949] AC 386 the defendants sold petrol to the claimant who was nine years old. The claimant was burned playing with it but it was held that he was not contributory negligent.

### Case precedent – *Gough v Thorne* [1966] 3 All ER 398

**Facts:** A 13 year old girl was waiting to cross a busy road. A lorry driver stopped and signalled to her to cross. As she was doing so a car overtook the lorry and hit the girl. The High Court found that she was contributory negligent. The Court of Appeal said that the lorry driver had beckoned to her to cross and she relied on him. She was not contributory negligent.

**Principle:** How should children be judged? Denning LJ said that, 'A very young child cannot be guilty of contributory negligence.' A child should only be contributorily negligent if they are 'of such age as to be expected to take precautions for his or her own safety'.

**Application:** The courts will lean in favour of children when determining their contribution. Young children are not likely to be contributory negligent.

The Supreme Court reviewed the application of the law in *Jackson v Murray* [2015] UKSC 5 . The claimant, a 13 year old girl, got off the school mini-bus one winter's evening in fading light and emerged from behind the bus to cross the road. The defendant was travelling towards the bus on the opposite side of the road. He was driving at 50 mph within the speed limit but too fast for the conditions and hit and injured her. At trial she was found 90% contributorily negligent and this was reduced to 70% on appeal. The Supreme Court said that the court below was wrong to say that the claimant was more responsible for the accident than the defendant. More responsibility is on drivers than pedestrians because cars can do more harm. The parties were equally responsible and damages were reduced by 50%.

## Emergencies

If the defendant negligently creates a danger and the claimant acts in the heat of the moment the courts will take this into account in judging the conduct of the claimant. If the claimant has acted reasonably they will not be treated as contributorily negligent. Compare the following two cases.

| *Jones v Boyce* (1816) 1 Stark 493 | *Holomis v Dubuc* [1975] 56 DLR (3d) 351 |
|---|---|
| The claimant was sitting on top of the defendant's horse-drawn coach as it was going downhill. A defective rein broke and the claimant, believing it would crash, jumped off and broke his leg. The coach did not crash. It was held that a reasonable and prudent person would have acted in the same way and the claimant was not contributory negligent. | The claimant was a passenger in a sea plane. The defendant was the pilot and he landed on a lake in the fog, hit an obstacle and the plane started to fill with water. Three passengers jumped out and one of them, the claimant's husband, drowned. It was held that jumping out in an emergency was not contributorily negligent but failing to put on the life belts which were available was. Damages were reduced by 50%. |

In *Sayers v Harlow UDC* [1958] 2 All ER 342 the claimant was waiting for a bus and went to the ladies' public toilets which were owned by the defendants. When she went to leave the cubicle she found that the door lock had jammed. After shouting and banging on the door for 15 minutes she tried to climb out. She put one foot on the toilet seat and one foot on the toilet roll holder, the toilet roll rotated and she slipped, fell and was injured. The Court of Appeal said that although it was reasonable to try and climb out she had done so in a careless manner and damages were reduced by 25%.

## The claimant's act caused some damage

The claimant's act must either partly cause the accident or must cause some of the damage. The harm to the claimant must be the kind of harm which is likely to happen from the claimant's careless act.

### Case precedent – *Froom v Butcher* [1976] QB 286

**Facts:** The claimant was in a car accident caused by the defendant's negligence. He was not wearing his seatbelt although this was not compulsory at that time. He suffered head injuries which he would not have suffered if he had been wearing a seatbelt.

**Principle:** It was held by the Court of Appeal that he had been contributorily negligent by not wearing his seatbelt and his damages were reduced by 20%.

**Application:** The guidelines set out by Lord Denning have been used by the courts ever since.

In *Froom* Lord Denning made an important distinction between the cause of the accident and the cause of the damage:

> 'But in seatbelt cases the cause of the accident is one thing. The cause of the damage is another. The accident is caused by the bad driving. The damage is caused in part by the bad driving of the defendant, and in part by the failure of the plaintiff to wear a seatbelt.'

| Lord Denning set out the following guidance for reduction in damages for not wearing a seatbelt: |
| --- |
| 0% if failure to wear a seatbelt made no difference to the injuries; |
| 15% if the injuries would have been less severe; |
| 25% if the injuries would have been prevented altogether. |
| These are guidelines and although they are usually followed they will not be followed in exceptional cases, for example, if wearing a seatbelt would have caused greater injuries. |

The guidelines were applied to cycle helmets in *Smith v Finch* [2009] EWHC 53 (QB). The claimant rode out of a side road on his bicycle and was hit by the defendant's motorcycle. The claimant suffered head injuries. The defendant argued that the claimant was contributory negligent because he was not wearing a cycle helmet. There is no legal requirement to wear a cycle helmet. It was held that on the evidence, in a collision at low speed, a helmet would have made no difference. The claimant was not contributorily negligent.

## Can someone be 100% contributory negligent?

In *Pitts v Hunt* [1990] 3 All ER 344 the claimant, aged 18, and the defendant, aged 16, spent the evening drinking. They then set off home on the defendant's moped. The claimant knew that the defendant was under age for riding, had no licence and no insurance. The defendant was weaving across the road to frighten people and the claimant encouraged him. The moped hit a car and the defendant was killed. The High Court said that the claimant was 100% contributory negligent. The Court of Appeal held that the LR(CN) Act 1945 assumes that the claimant will recover some damages and it was illogical to make him 100% contributory negligent.

### Common Pitfall

When determining who caused the damage in negligence one issue may be whether the claimant's act was a new intervening act. If it is determined it does not amount to that an alternative is that the claimant is contributory negligent.

# Consent

The defence of consent is also known as *volenti non fit injuria* which means no wrong is done to someone who consents. If the claimant consents to the defendant's act then the defendant is not liable. The defence provides a complete defence.

Two requirements are needed to establish the defence of consent.

## Knowledge of the risk

A person cannot consent to a risk if they do not know about it. The claimant must know the nature and extent of the risk. Knowledge of the risk in itself is not enough for consent and the claimant's conduct must show that they accept the risk. If the claimant acts unreasonably this may be treated as consent. There may be an agreement by the claimant to accept the risk but this would be unusual.

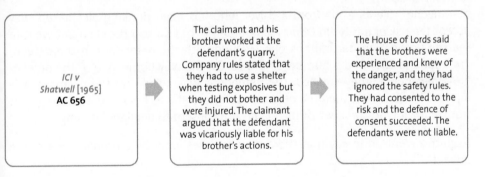

## Voluntary consent to the risk

The claimant must have full knowledge of the risks and the claimant's consent must be voluntary. The test for consent is subjective – has this particular claimant consented rather than an objective test of a reasonable person. In *Smith v Baker* [1891] AC 325 the claimant worked for the defendant building a railway. A crane repeatedly swung rocks over his head in a crate and he had complained about this but continued working. A rock fell from the crate and injured him. The defendant argued that he had consented. The House of Lords said that he had not acted voluntarily and had not consented to the risk. He had no real choice but to keep working.

## Suicide

If the defendant is under a duty to prevent someone committing suicide but that person does so, can the defendant use the defence of consent? In *Reeves v Commissioner of Police of the Metropolis* [2000] 1 AC 360 a prisoner, who was a known suicide risk but of sound mind, hanged himself. The defendants claimed the defence of consent. The House of Lords said that given the circumstances that the defendants had control over the prisoner and the risk of prisoners committing suicide they were under a duty to prevent the prisoner committing suicide. The defence of consent failed but the prisoner was found 50% contributory negligent.

### Common Pitfall

If the defence of consent cannot be established in a particular situation remember to consider the alternative defence of contributory negligence.

## Rescuers

If a rescuer goes to help someone in danger, for example, in a traffic accident, does the rescuer consent to the risk of harm? The law does not normally treat the rescuer as voluntarily consenting to the risks. This applies to both professional and lay rescuers. In *Haynes v Harwood* [1935] 1 KB 146 a police officer who was injured stopping a horse-drawn van in a busy street was not regarded as consenting to the risks.

## Drinking cases

If someone accepts a lift from a driver who has been drinking alcohol do they accept the risk of injury? In *Dann v Hamilton* [1939] 1 KB 509 the claimant went to see the Coronation decorations one evening with the defendant in the defendant's car and they had a number of drinks. On the way home, due to the defendant's negligence, they crashed, the defendant was killed and the claimant was injured. The claimant sued the defendant's estate. It was held that accepting a lift from a driver who had been drinking was not consent to negligent driving.

Asquith J went on to say that there may be cases where the drunkenness of the driver is:

'so extreme and so glaring that to accept a lift from him is like engaging in an intrinsically and obviously dangerous occupation, intermeddling with an unexploded bomb or walking on the edge of an unfenced cliff.'

The Road Traffic Act 1988 s149 provides that the defence of consent cannot be used in road traffic cases where vehicles are required to be insured.

The principles from *Dann v Hamilton* were applied in the next case.

> **Case precedent – *Morris v Murray* [1990] 3 All ER 801**
>
> **Facts:** The claimant and defendant spent the afternoon drinking and the defendant had the equivalent of 17 whiskies. The defendant then suggested going flying in his small plane and the claimant drove them to the airfield and helped to start the plane. It crashed killing the defendant and injuring the claimant.
>
> **Principle:** The Court of Appeal said that the claimant knew the defendant had drunk a considerable amount and the claimant had consented to the risk.
>
> **Application:** Although consent is not available in road traffic cases it can apply in other cases like this. One difficult line to draw is deciding when someone is too drunk to consent to the risk. The claimant in this case must have just been able to consent.

## Exclusion notices

The defendant may attempt to exclude liability by a contractual term or a notice. These used to be governed by the Unfair Contract Terms Act 1977 but are now covered by the Consumer Rights Act 2015. The CRA distinguishes between consumer contracts made between an individual and a trader and other contracts. Under s65(1) 'A trader cannot by the term of a consumer contract or consumer notice exclude or restrict liability for death or personal injury resulting from negligence.' Under s65(2) 'a person is not to be taken as having accepted any risk merely because they agreed to or knew about the term or notice'.

The effect is that someone acting in the course of a business cannot exclude liability for death or injury arising from their negligence. However, private individuals may still exclude liability between one another.

# Illegality

A person cannot bring a claim in tort if they suffer harm while carrying out an illegal act. This principle is known as *ex turpi causa non oritur actio*, which means that no action can be based on an illegal act. It is also known as the defence of illegality.

The rule is based loosely on public policy that someone should not be able to claim compensation for the consequences of their criminal acts. However, the exact basis of the rule and how it applies in practice has caused difficulties for the courts. There are two factors which are relevant to the defence:

❖ public policy;
❖ causation – involving the extent to which the claimant's illegal act has caused the claimant's injuries.

A clear example of the operation of the principle is *Ashton v Turner* [1981] QB 137. When the claimant and defendant were driving away from a burglary, due to the defendant's negligent driving, they crashed and the claimant was injured. The claimant's action failed because at the time of his injury he was involved in a crime.

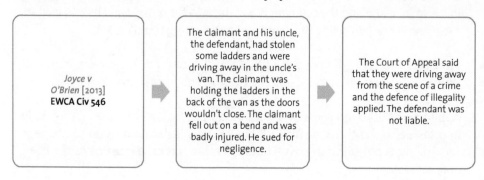

In *Gray v Thames Trains Ltd* [2009] UKHL 33 the claimant suffered post-traumatic stress disorder (PTSD) in a train accident caused by the defendant's negligence. Sometime later because of his condition he killed someone, was convicted of manslaughter and detained in a secure hospital for an indefinite period. He sued for damages for PTSD and for loss of earnings while he was detained. The House of Lords held that he was entitled to compensation only up to the time of his conviction. At that point the defence of illegality applied.

Compare the decisions in the following cases.

| *McCracken v Smith & others* [2015] EWCA Civ 380 | *Smith v Stratton and another* [2015] EWCA Civ 1413 |
|---|---|
| The defendant stole a trials bike and was carrying the claimant as a pillion passenger. The bike collided with a minibus negligently driven by DB. The claimant and defendant were both badly injured and the claimant sued for negligence.<br><br>The Court of Appeal said that the claimant and defendant were parties to a joint criminal enterprise of riding the bike dangerously. The accident was caused by the dangerous driving of the bike and the negligent driving of the minibus. The criminal conduct involved in one cause was not enough for the defence of *ex turpi causa* to apply.<br><br>The claim against the defendant and DB succeeded. However, the claimant's damages were reduced by 65% to reflect his contribution including 15% for his failure to wear a helmet. | The claimant was a passenger in a car driven by the defendant, which crashed when chased by a police car and the claimant was injured. The defendant's insurance was invalid and the Motor Insurers Bureau was the second defendant. The four men in the car were involved in dealing in cannabis and the accident happened when they drove away to avoid being caught.<br><br>The Court of Appeal said that this was a joint criminal enterprise and the defence of *ex turpi causa* applied. |

The limits of the illegality defence were shown in *Revill v Newberry* [1996] 1 All ER 291. The defendant, an old man, slept in his allotment shed to protect his property. He heard the claimant trying to break in and shot him through a hole in the door. The defendant put forward the defence of illegality. The court said that the defendant did owe a duty to the claimant and could not treat him as an outlaw. The defence of illegality failed.

# Limitation

The law sets time limits for bringing claims in civil law. It would be unjust to allow claims many years after a tort was committed and it would raise issues of the reliability of evidence. The law is set out in the Limitation Act 1980 as amended.

| | Limitation Act 1980 |
|---|---|
| s2 | The general rule is that claims in tort must be brought within six years of when the cause of action arises.<br><br>❖ If a tort requires proof of damage the cause of action arises when the damage occurs, e.g. negligence.<br>❖ If a tort is actionable *per se* and does not require proof of damage the cause of action arises when the defendant commits the tort, e.g. trespass to the person. |
| s11 | *But* claims for personal injury due to negligence, nuisance or breach of duty must be brought within three years from when:<br><br>(a) the right of action arises; or<br>(b) the date the claimant has knowledge of the injury. |
| s14 | The date of knowledge is when the claimant first had knowledge:<br><br>❖ the injury was significant;<br>❖ the injury was caused wholly or partly by the act or omission of the defendant (negligence, nuisance or breach of statutory duty);<br>❖ of the identity of the defendant;<br>❖ if the act was by someone apart from the defendant the identity of that other person.<br><br>A claimant will be treated as having knowledge which the claimant would be able to obtain with or without professional help. |
| s4A | Provides that the normal six-year period does not apply to defamation and the claim must be brought within one year.<br><br>Under s8 Defamation Act 2013 if there is a later publication of the same defamation the time limit is one year from the date of the first publication. |
| s1 | Death – Law Reform (Miscellaneous Provisions) Act 1934<br>If a claimant dies as a result of a tort, before the end of the three-year period, their dependants have three years from the date of the claimant's death in which to sue. |

## Extending the limitation period

Under s33 the court has a discretion to extend the limitation period and will take all the circumstances into account including:

(a) the length of the delay by the claimant and the reasons;
(b) the effect of the delay on the evidence of the claimant or defendant;
(c) the conduct of the defendant after the claim arose including responding to the claimant;
(d) the duration of any disability of the claimant arising after the claim arose;
(e) whether the claimant acted promptly once they knew they could sue;
(f) the steps taken by the claimant to obtain medical, legal or other advice.

This section only applied to claims under s11 and did not cover torts actionable *per se*. The law was changed in *A v Hoare* [2008] UKHL 6 in which the claimant sued for trespass 16 years after she was raped by the defendant. The reason she sued after this time was that the defendant had recently won £7 million on the Lottery. Under s2 Limitation Act 1980 she had six years in which to claim but this period had passed. The House of Lords said that a claim for personal injury from an intentional trespass was within s11. As a result the court could extend the period under s33 and allow her claim.

## Aim Higher

Read the article, 'Time to Take Time' by R Scorer, 2016, NLJ 7693 p10.

This examines the problems caused by the Limitation Acts for people bringing claims for historical sex abuse and how to deal with those problems.

It also looks at how Scotland, Australia and Canada are dealing with similar problems.

# Putting it into practice

Read the scenario below and answer the question.

Bonnie was driving into town with Clyde intending to rob a jeweller's shop in the Wessex Shopping Centre. Bonnie was driving too fast, lost control of the car on a bend and skidded across the road. The car knocked over Daisy, a 14 year old schoolgirl, who was crossing the road whilst texting on her mobile phone and crashed into a lamp post. Daisy was seriously injured.

Clyde suffered head injuries in the accident. When the police arrived they found that Clyde had a quantity of cannabis in his pocket. Twelve months later Clyde shot someone dead during a robbery. He was subsequently convicted of manslaughter and sent to prison for five years.

Eva, who was shopping at the Wessex Shopping Centre, went to the public toilets which are owned by Wessex Council. When she tried to leave the toilet cubicle she found that the lock had jammed. She banged on the toilet door and shouted for five minutes but no one heard her. She then broke the toilet window and tried to climb out but in doing so was cut on broken glass.

**Advise Daisy, Clyde and Eva of the claims they may make in negligence and the defences which may be available to those claims.**

# Outline answer – negligence, illegality, consent and contributory negligence

❖ *Daisy*

     ❖ Daisy v Bonnie: duty of care in negligence, both road users; breach of duty, Bonnie driving too fast, test of a competent driver; 'but for' test, would Daisy have been injured but for Bonnie's careless driving? No; consider if Daisy is a cause of the accident.

     ❖ Is Daisy partly to blame? Contributory negligence; Law Reform (Contributory Negligence) Act 1945 damages may be reduced as the court thinks just and equitable; in *Jackson v Murray* the Supreme Court said that a car can do more harm than a pedestrian; in applying this it is likely Daisy will only be a small percentage to blame.

❖ *Clyde*

     ❖ Clyde v Bonnie: negligence; duty of care to other road users including passengers; breach of duty by Bonnie; causation, 'but for' test applies; would Clyde have been injured but for Bonnie's negligent driving? No; Bonnie liable in negligence.

     ❖ Consent: not available in road traffic claims, RT Act 1988 s149.

     ❖ Illegality: *ex turpi causa*; is Clyde's claim based on an illegal act? The first issue is the fact they are on the way to commit a crime. In *Ashton v Turner* the claimant was being driven away from a burglary which was seen as being involved in committing a crime; Clyde's position can be distinguished as he is merely on his way to commit a crime.

     ❖ The second issue is the cannabis: in *Smith v Stratton* the car was being used to deal in cannabis; does Clyde only have a small amount?

     ❖ Could Clyde claim for being sent to prison and his loss of earnings in prison? In *Gray v Thames Trains* the claimant could not be given damages after he was sent to prison because he was responsible for the killing. In Clyde's case as he carried out robberies he may at some point have killed someone anyway.

❖ *Eva*

     ❖ Eva v Wessex Council: negligence; duty of care to maintain toilet lock; breach of duty by not checking; 'but for' test, if not for the breach Eva would not have been locked in the toilet and injured.

     ❖ Emergency, *Sayers v Harlow UDC* damages reduced 25%; application here: did Eva wait long enough? Was her action reasonable? Under the LR(CN) Act 1945 her damages may be reduced by a small percentage.

     ❖ Could Eva breaking the window come within *ex turpi causa*? Unlikely as Eva is trying to escape from a situation caused by negligence.

# Table of key cases referred to in this chapter

| Key case | Area of law | Principle |
|---|---|---|
| *Froom v Butcher* [1976] QB 286 | The claimant suffered head injuries in a car accident but would not have done if he had worn a seatbelt. | Damages were reduced by 20%. If the claimant is partly to blame for their injuries the court can reduce damages on the basis of what is just and equitable. |
| *ICI v Shatwell* [1965] AC 656 | Two brothers were injured testing explosives because they did not use the shelter provided by their employer. | The House of Lords said that they had consented as they were experienced and knew the risks. |
| *Jackson v Murray* [2015] UKSC 5 | A 13 year old girl crossing the road from behind a mini-bus was hit by the defendant driver. The Supreme Court held that the parties were equally to blame and damages were reduced by 50%. | A motorist carries more responsibility than a pedestrian. |
| *Joyce v O'Brien* [2013] EWCA Civ 546 | The claimant fell out of the back of the defendant's van as they drove off with stolen ladders. | The defendant could rely on the defence of *ex turpi causa* as they were in the course of committing a crime. |
| *McCracken v Smith* [2015] EWCA Civ 380 | The claimant was injured when the stolen trials bike he was on was hit by the defendant's negligently driven minibus. | The Court of Appeal held that the criminal conduct in one cause, riding the stolen bike, was not enough for *ex turpi causa* to apply. But the claimant was contributory negligent. |
| *Morris v Murray* [1990] 3 All ER 801 | The claimant was injured when the defendant's plane crashed after they had spent the afternoon drinking. | The Court of Appeal said that the claimant and accepted the risks and the defence of consent applied. |
| *Pitts v Hunt* [1990] 3 All ER 344 | The claimant and defendant spent the evening drinking and then set off on the defendant's moped. They crashed and the claimant was injured. | The Court of Appeal said that the claimant could not be held 100% contributory negligent as the LR(CN) Act 1945 presumes that the claimant will be entitled to some damages. |

@ **Visit the book's companion website to test your knowledge**

❖ Resources include a subject map, revision tip podcasts, downloadable diagrams, MCQ quizzes for each chapter and a flashcard glossary

❖ www.routledge.com/cw/optimizelawrevision

# 11

# Remedies

## Revision objectives

**Understand the law**

- Can you distinguish between general and specific damages giving examples to illustrate?
- Can you explain the purpose of compensatory damages and name the four types?
- Can you identify the three claims which may arise if the victim of a tort dies?
- Can you name and explain the two main types of injunction?

**Remember the details**

- Can you explain what claims may be made under the heading of pecuniary losses?
- Can you explain the basis of a claim under the Fatal Accidents Act 1976 and list those who can make a claim?
- Can you distinguish between an interim injunction and a *quia timet* injunction?

**Reflect critically on areas of debate**

- Can you explain the role of bereavement damages and consider whether the law should be changed?

**Contextualise**

- Do you understand how remedies are relevant to problem questions?
- Do you understand the importance of injunctions in continuing torts like nuisance and defamation?

**Apply your skills and knowledge**

- Can you answer the question at the end of this chapter?

# Chapter Map

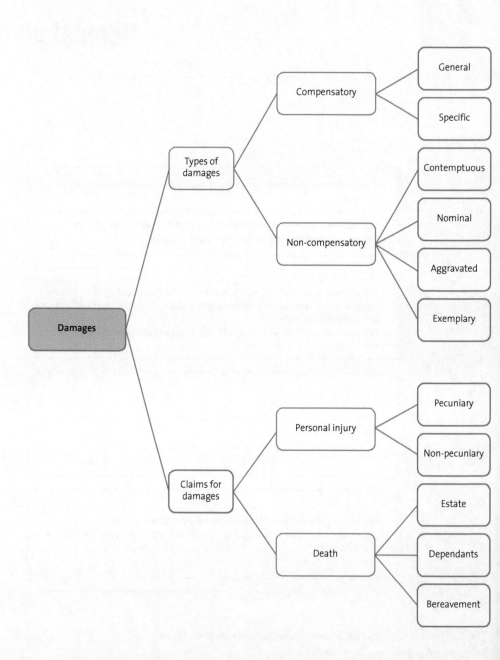

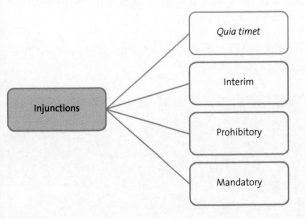

# Introduction

The two main remedies in tort are damages and injunctions. Damages are simply money compensation. Injunctions are court orders mainly to stop the defendant continuing with the tort. There are also specific remedies which apply to individual torts in addition to these two remedies.

| Damages | Injunctions |
|---|---|
| For loss, injury and death | To stop the tort |

# Damages

Damages are compensation for the claimant. The main aim of damages in tort is to put the claimant in the position they would have been in if the tort had not been committed. Damages can also be given for torts which do not need the claimant to prove any damage, for example, battery.

A claimant is under a duty to mitigate their losses, which means they must take reasonable steps to reduce their losses.

> ## Common Pitfall
>
> Remember the distinction.
>
> 'Damages' is the legal term for money compensation. 'Damage' is the legal term for the harm suffered by the claimant, for example in a road traffic accident.

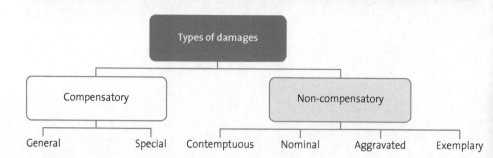

Types of damages

- Compensatory
  - General
  - Special
- Non-compensatory
  - Contemptuous
  - Nominal
  - Aggravated
  - Exemplary

## Compensatory

The purpose of compensatory damages is to compensate the claimant for the loss they have suffered. Although the aim is to put the claimant in their original position before the tort, this will not always be possible especially if the claimant has suffered personal injuries, for example, losing a leg in a car accident caused by the defendant's negligence. Damages are the only means to provide some compensation.

## General damages

General damages are damages which cannot be precisely measured in money terms, for example, damages for pain, suffering and loss of future earnings.

## Special damages

Special damages are those damages which can be precisely measured, for example, loss of earnings up to the date of the trial, replacement cost of a dress ruined in an accident.

# Non-compensatory damages

## Contemptuous

This is a very small sum, usually the lowest coin in use, which is one penny. The court is saying that although there has been a technical breach of the law the claimant should not have brought the case to court. Such awards have been given in defamation cases in the past but following the Defamation Act 2013 s1 the claimant must now prove serious harm.

## Nominal

This is a small sum of money awarded where the defendant has committed a tort but the claimant has not suffered any damage. Nominal damages could be awarded for torts actionable *per se* (without proof of damage) like trespass to land, for example, £5.

## Aggravated

If the defendant has behaved in a malicious way in committing the tort or dealing with the claimant which has caused mental distress or injury to the claimant's feelings, the court may award aggravated damages. They are not available for negligence but usually only for intentional torts. In *Rowlands v Chief Constable of Merseyside* [2006] EWCA Civ 1773 the Court of Appeal awarded aggravated damages of £7,000 to the claimant who was wrongly arrested in a humiliating manner in front of her children. She was also awarded exemplary damages.

## Exemplary

The purpose of exemplary damages is to punish the defendant. In *Rookes v Barnard* [1964] AC 1129 the House of Lords said that such damages could only be awarded if:

❖ there was oppressive, arbitrary or unconstitutional action by Government servants, for example, they are abusing their power; or
❖ a defendant has committed a tort and calculated that they will make a profit from it. In *Cassell v Broome* [1972] AC 1027 Cassell published a book wrongly accusing Broome of being responsible for the sinking of a convoy in the Second World War believing they would make more money from it than any damages awarded. Broome was awarded £25,000 exemplary damages.

## Common Pitfall

Aggravated damages are extra damages awarded for the mental distress caused by the way the defendant has acted in committing the tort. They are still to compensate the claimant.

This is in contrast to exemplary damages which are given to punish the claimant.

## Claims for personal injury

Claims for damages for physical and psychiatric injury are more difficult to assess than claims for damage to property. In the case of property damage the claimant will be entitled to the replacement cost or the cost of repair. Losses for personal injury can be divided into pecuniary (or financial) loss and non-pecuniary loss.

| Pecuniary losses | Non-pecuniary losses |
|---|---|
| • Reasonable expenses, e.g. private medical expenses are allowed<br>• Loss of earnings up to the trial<br>• Loss of future earnings multiplicand (annual net earnings) × multiplier (number of years that loss will continue)<br>• Loss of earning capacity, e.g. if claimant has to take a lower paid job<br>• If life is shortened, a claim for 'lost years' the claimant would have worked<br>• Cost of a carer if necessary, either professional or family | • Pain, suffering and loss of amenity (PSLA)<br>• Pain from the injury and the medical treatment<br>• Suffering is separate to pain and is for the distress and disruption to life caused by the injury<br>• Loss of amenity is a claim for not being able to live life to the full after the accident, e.g. no longer able to play sports or enjoy previous leisure interests, or personal relationships |

In determining the loss of future earnings the courts take the contingencies of life into account, for example, the claimant may become ill, may be made redundant, may be promoted etc. Consequently they work on a maximum of 18 years for the multiplier. In *Howitt v Heads* [1972] 1 All ER 491 a claim was made by a 21 year old widow under the Fatal Accidents Act 1976 for the loss of income of her husband for 40 years. The court used a multiplier of 18 times her husband's salary.

## Deductions

A claimant may receive financial compensation following an accident which does not come from the defendant. The courts do not wish claimants to be compensated twice and some of these extra benefits will be deducted from the damages paid while others will not be deducted. If the claimant has been given money by a charity or from an insurance policy this can be kept. But sick pay from an employer and social security payments including sickness benefit will be deducted. Under the Social Security (Recovery of Benefits) Act 1997 s6 any benefits paid in the five years after the accident or until compensation is paid, whichever is the earliest, will be deducted from the damages.

# Death

### Claim by the estate

* ❖ A person's estate is what they leave on death.
* ❖ If the claimant dies before the claim reaches court under the Law Reform (Miscellaneous Provisions) Act 1934 s1(1) all claims by or against the estate survive for the benefit of the estate.
* ❖ The exception is claims for defamation.
* ❖ Whoever inherits the estate can claim for the losses up to the death.
* ❖ They claim as the representative of the deceased.
* ❖ The claim covers pecuniary and non-pecuniary losses.

### Claim by the dependants of the deceased

* ❖ This is a separate claim.
* ❖ If someone dies as a result of a tort anyone who was financially dependent on the deceased may make a claim against the defendant under the Fatal Accidents Act 1976 s1. This is a claim by the dependant for the loss they have suffered as a result of the death caused by the defendant.
* ❖ The list of dependants is set out under s1(3) and includes:

    * ❖ spouse or former spouse;
    * ❖ civil partner or former civil partner;
    * ❖ anyone who has lived with the deceased for two years before death as a spouse or civil partner;
    * ❖ parents or anyone treated as parents;
    * ❖ the deceased's children including anyone treated as a child of the family;
    * ❖ children of any brother, sister, uncle or aunt of the deceased;
    * ❖ stepchildren;
    * ❖ illegitimate children.

* ❖ The person claiming must show that they were financially dependent on the deceased.

### Bereavement damages

* ❖ The Fatal Accidents Act 1976 s1A provides for damages to be paid for bereavement. This is a fixed sum of £12,980.
* ❖ Claims may be made only by:

    * ❖ the spouse or civil partner of the deceased;
    * ❖ the parents of a minor who was never married or in a civil partnership; and
    * ❖ if the child is illegitimate the mother only.

# Injunctions

An injunction is a court order stopping the defendant from doing something or ordering the defendant to do a particular act.

An injunction is an equitable remedy and will only be granted at the discretion of the court. It will not be given if damages are an adequate remedy.

Failure to obey an injunction is contempt of court which is a criminal offence.

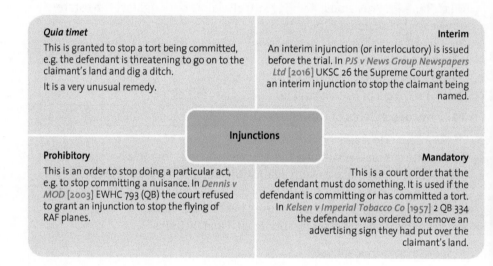

**Quia timet**

This is granted to stop a tort being committed, e.g. the defendant is threatening to go on to the claimant's land and dig a ditch.

It is a very unusual remedy.

**Interim**

An interim injunction (or interlocutory) is issued before the trial. In *PJS v News Group Newspapers Ltd* [2016] UKSC 26 the Supreme Court granted an interim injunction to stop the claimant being named.

**Injunctions**

**Prohibitory**

This is an order to stop doing a particular act, e.g. to stop committing a nuisance. In *Dennis v MOD* [2003] EWHC 793 (QB) the court refused to grant an injunction to stop the flying of RAF planes.

**Mandatory**

This is a court order that the defendant must do something. It is used if the defendant is committing or has committed a tort. In *Kelsen v Imperial Tobacco Co* [1957] 2 QB 334 the defendant was ordered to remove an advertising sign they had put over the claimant's land.

# Putting it into practice

Answer the following question.

Ann is 50 years old and is a company director in the city earning £50,000 per year. She owns a detached house where she lives with her husband Bill who does not work but looks after the house. Six months ago Ann was standing at the bus stop one morning when a car mounted the pavement and knocked her over. Daljit, the driver, was speeding as he was late for work. Ann broke her arm in the crash and her leather coat was badly torn. Ann's arm was so badly damaged it needed a number of operations to rebuild it and she has been told it will be 12 months from the accident until she can work again.

Ann had an accident insurance policy which has paid her half her salary for six months but that has now stopped. She has also been claiming state benefits. Ann will not be able to continue with her company job. She was also a keen tennis player but is no longer able to play because of her injuries.

Her neighbour, Eric, has recently formed a rock band. He practices three days a week often starting in the afternoons until late at night. As Ann is at home convalescing the noise is driving her mad. She has complained to Eric but he has continued to practice.

**Advise Ann of the remedies she may have against Daljit and Eric in respect of the above torts.**

**Assuming Ann was killed in the accident explain what claims may be made.**

# Outline answer – damages and injunction

❖ Identify legal issues and apply the law

❖ *Daljit and the crash*

  ❖ Define negligence; one party owes a duty of care to another, *Caparo* test; Daljit owes a duty to Ann another road user. Daljit is in breach of duty; *Nettleship v Weston* [1971] 3 All ER 581; the breach has caused the harm to Ann; 'but for' test; Ann will succeed in a negligence claim.

  ❖ Claim for personal injuries: identify claims for pecuniary and non-pecuniary loss.

  ❖ Pecuniary losses: loss of earnings up to the date of the trial which will be the net amount.

  ❖ Loss of future earnings is more difficult to calculate and will be her net annual earnings multiplied by the number of years the court determine; assuming she has approximately 15 years working left, the court may award one-third of this time or less as the multiplier × net salary.

  ❖ Ann will have to take a lower paid job and she can claim for loss of earning capacity.

  ❖ Her coat: likely to be the replacement cost.

  ❖ Non-pecuniary loss: this is a claim for pain, suffering and loss of amenity (PSLA); the pain of the initial injury and for the operations she has had or will need in the future; she can also claim damages for suffering for the disruption to her life; and for loss of amenity, as she can no longer play tennis.

❖ *Eric and the noise*

  ❖ Identify the legal basis of Ann's claim, private nuisance; the noise is an indirect act interfering with her enjoyment of land; test of reasonableness; factors like if it is a quiet area etc. *Sturges v Bridgman* (1879) 11 Ch 852; is Ann sensitive as she is convalescing?

  ❖ Ann has an interest in land as she owns the house; she has a strong claim.

  ❖ Remedies: damages; and a prohibitory injunction to stop Eric continuing with his music; may be made subject to conditions as to the time he can play, *Kennaway v Thompson* [1980] 3 All ER 329.

❖ *If Ann was killed in the accident*

    ❖ Claim by the estate; under the Law Reform (Miscellaneous Provisions) Act 1934 s1(1) the claim against Daljit survives for the benefit of the estate; assuming Bill inherits the estate he can claim on behalf of Ann for the losses specified above.

    ❖ Claim by dependants: under the Fatal Accidents Act 1976 s1 anyone financially dependent on the deceased can make a claim and this includes a spouse; Bill is her spouse and was dependent on Ann, he can claim for loss of income.

    ❖ Bereavement damages: he can also claim bereavement damages of £12,980.

# Table of key cases referred to in this chapter

| Key case | Area of law | Principle |
|---|---|---|
| *Cassell v Broome* [1972] AC 1027 | Cassell published libels about Broome knowing that they were wrong and hoping to make a profit over any libel payments. | Broome awarded exemplary damages to punish Cassell. |
| *Dennis v MOD* [2003] EWHC 793 (QB) | The noise of planes from an RAF base was a nuisance. Claimant awarded damages. | An injunction to stop flying was refused as public benefit outweighed private rights. |
| *PJS v Newsgroup Newspapers Ltd* [2016] UKSC 26 | The married claimant had a sexual relationship and wished to keep it private until the hearing for breach of confidence came to court. | The Supreme Court granted an interim injunction even though the claimant's name was published on the internet in other countries. It would keep the national press from revealing it. |
| *Rowlands v Chief Constable of Merseyside* [2006] EWCA Civ 1773 | The claimant was wrongly arrested in a humiliating manner and sued the police for false imprisonment. | The Court of Appeal awarded the claimant aggravated damages because of the behaviour of the police officers. |

---

@ **Visit the book's companion website to test your knowledge**

❖ Resources include a subject map, revision tip podcasts, downloadable diagrams, MCQ quizzes for each chapter and a flashcard glossary

❖ www.routledge.com/cw/optimizelawrevision

# Index